From Your Friends at **The MAILBOX**®

Animals

Grades 4–6

INVESTIGATING SCIENCE

Project Manager:
Cindy Mondello

Writers:
Daniel Kriesberg, Linda Manwiller, Stephanie Willett-Smith

Editors:
Cayce Guiliano, Peggy Hambright, Deborah T. Kalwat,
Scott Lyons, Jennifer Munnerlyn

Art Coordinator:
Clevell Harris

Artists:
Theresa Lewis Goode, Clevell Harris, Rob Mayworth,
Greg D. Rieves

Cover Artists:
Nick Greenwood and Kimberly Richard

www.themailbox.com

©2000 by THE EDUCATION CENTER, INC.
All rights reserved.
ISBN #1-56234-410-2

Manufactured in the United States

10 9 8 7 6 5 4 3 2

Table of Contents

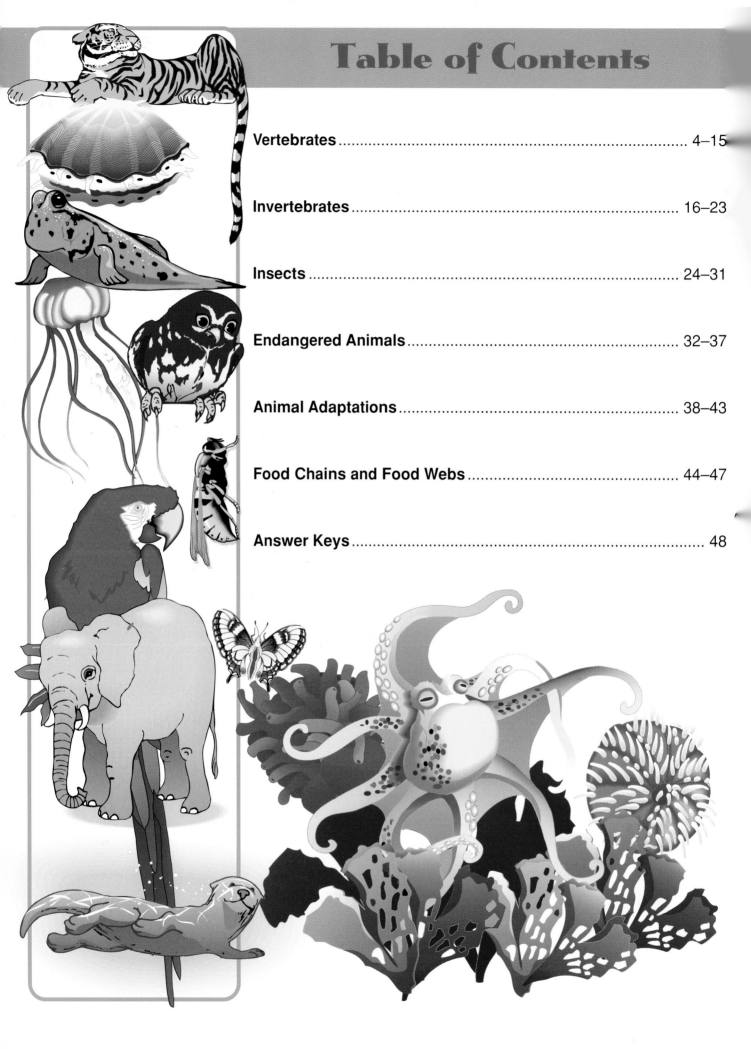

About This Book

Welcome to *Investigating Science—Animals*! This book is one of eight must-have resource books that support the National Science Education Standards and are designed to supplement and enhance your existing science curriculum. Packed with practical cross-curricular ideas and thought-provoking reproducibles, these all-new, content-specific resource books provide intermediate teachers with a collection of innovative and fun activities for teaching thematic science units.

Included in this book:

Investigating Science—Animals contains six cross-curricular thematic units, each containing

- Background information for the teacher
- Easy-to-implement instructions for science experiments and projects
- Student-centered activities and reproducibles
- Literature links

Cross-curricular thematic units found in this book:

- *Vertebrates*
- *Invertebrates*
- *Insects*
- *Endangered Animals*
- *Animal Adaptations*
- *Food Chains and Food Webs*

Other books in the intermediate Investigating Science series:

- *Investigating Science—Space*
- *Investigating Science—Weather & Climate*
- *Investigating Science—Plants*
- *Investigating Science—The Earth*
- *Investigating Science—The Human Body*
- *Investigating Science—Light & Sound*
- *Investigating Science—Energy, Magnetism, & Machines*

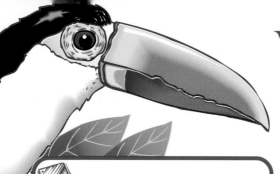

Vertebrates

Use the following activities and reproducibles to help your students learn valuable information about the varied world of vertebrates.

Background for the Teacher

Vertebrates are animals with backbones. There are about 40,000 species of vertebrates. They are divided into eight classes, including *birds, fish, reptiles, amphibians,* and *mammals.*

Mammals...
- are warm-blooded, and most are covered with hair or fur
- give birth to live young and feed young their milk

Birds...
- are warm-blooded and covered with feathers
- can be found in almost every environment around the world

Amphibians...
- are cold-blooded animals
- live in water when they are young and move to land when they are grown
- are divided into three groups: frogs and toads; newts, salamanders, and sirens; and caecilians (wormlike creatures)

Reptiles...
- are cold-blooded animals covered with scales
- lay eggs, and most live in warm or hot climates
- are divided into four groups: lizards and snakes, turtles and tortoises, crocodilians, and tuatara (a lizardlike reptile, in its own group, that is the oldest species of reptile)

Fish...
- are cold-blooded animals that live in seas, oceans, ponds, rivers, and lakes
- (most) are covered with scales and use gills to breathe

Vertebrate Class Acts
(Research, Geography)

Give your students the opportunity to practice their world geography skills while learning about five of the eight classes of vertebrates. Begin by sharing the background information at the left with students. Next, divide your students into five groups and assign each group a vertebrate class: mammals, fish, reptiles, amphibians, or birds. Provide each group with a 5" x 25" strip of different-colored tagboard and markers or crayons. Explain to each group that vertebrates can be found in many parts of the world. Direct the group to use encyclopedias and other resource materials to find out where members of its class are located. Have the group find two vertebrates in its class in each of the categories shown below. Then instruct the group to make a chart and add pictures to its tagboard piece as shown. Display each group's chart on a bulletin board or wall, one above the other, to form one large chart. Encourage your students to refer to the information about each class throughout their study of vertebrates.

MAMMALS

N. America	S. America	Africa	Asia	Europe	Australia	Arctic	Oceans/lakes,etc
1. star-nosed mole	1. sloth	1. zebra	1. flying lemur	1. badger	1. koala	1. polar bear	1. dolphin
2. Alaskan fur seal	2. jaguar	2. giraffe	2. Kitti's hog-nosed bat	2. alpine marmot	2. kangaroo	2. Arctic fox	2. blue whale

FISH

N. America	S. America	Africa	Asia	Europe	Australia	Arctic	Oceans/lakes,etc.

Books With a Backbone

Amphibians (Our Living World series) by Edward R. Ricciuti (Blackbirch Press, Inc.; 1993)
Birds and How They Live (See and Explore series) by David Burnie (Dorling Kindersley Publishing, Inc.; 1999)
Frogs Swallow With Their Eyes! Weird Facts About Frogs, Snakes, Turtles, and Lizards by Melvin and Gilda Berger (Scholastic Inc., 1996)
Mind-Blowing Mammals (Amazing Animals series) by Leslee Elliott (Sterling Publishing Company, Inc.; 1994)
Reptile (Eyewitness Books series) by Colin McCarthy (Alfred A. Knopf, Inc.; 1991)
4 *What Is a Fish?* (The Science of Living Things series) by Bobbie Kalman and Allison Larin (Crabtree Publishing Company, 1999)

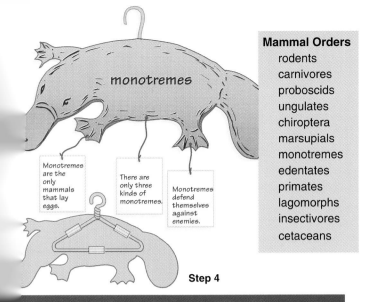

monotremes

Monotremes are the only mammals that lay eggs.

There are only three kinds of monotremes.

Monotremes defend themselves against enemies.

Step 4

Mammal Orders

rodents
carnivores
proboscids
ungulates
chiroptera
marsupials
monotremes
edentates
primates
lagomorphs
insectivores
cetaceans

The Class Will Come to Order
(Research, Art Activity)

Use this activity to help students learn about the many types and characteristics of the main mammal orders. Explain that of the more than 4,000 species of mammals, each belongs to an *order,* or a group, with which it shares certain characteristics. For example, all mammal species that belong to the order *carnivore*—such as tigers, wolves, and weasels—eat meat. Pair students and assign each pair one of the mammal orders from the list above. Direct the pair to research three or more facts about its assigned order. Then have the pair make a mobile about its order by providing the materials listed and a copy of the directions below.

Materials for each pair:
1 metal clothes hanger, 2 sheets of 12" x 18" construction paper, 3 different-sized lengths of yarn or string, three 4" x 5" construction paper pieces, 2 or 3 sheets of tissue paper, hole puncher, stapler, scissors, tape, and markers or crayons

Directions:
1. Draw the outline of an animal species from your order on one sheet of construction paper. (The animal needs to be large enough to cover the hanger.)
2. Place the other sheet of construction paper under your outlined page and cut out a back and front shape of your animal.
3. Write the order name in the center of the animal cutout. Decorate the cutout using markers or crayons.
4. Tape the hanger (representing the mammal's backbone) on the inside of the back animal shape as shown. Then place the front animal shape over the hanger and staple around the edges, leaving an opening near the top of the hanger. Next, stuff the animal with the tissue paper and staple it closed.
5. Punch three holes along the bottom edge of the animal shape and one hole in the top of each construction paper piece.
6. Write your facts on the front and back sides of the construction paper pieces. Use lengths of yarn to attach the cards to the animal as shown.

Who Wants to Be a "Mammal-aire"?
(Assessment, Review)

Mammal mania is sure to sweep through your class-room after your students play this fun, fact-filled game. Ahead of time, prepare 20 questions based on your study of mammals. Assign each question a dolphin dollar amount based on its level of difficulty. Then write the question in multiple-choice format on a transparency (Figure 1). Next, make an enlarged copy of the Life Savers pattern shown for each student (Figure 2). Then make a dolphin dollar amount chart on the chalkboard (Figure 3). To play the game, follow the directions below. As play continues, use the chart to help you keep track of each team's progress. Extend this activity by providing each student with a copy of the reproducible on page 11.

Directions:
1. Divide students into two teams.
2. Give each team member a copy of the Life Savers pattern. Explain to each student that she can use each of the three Life Saver statements only once per game. Instruct her to mark off each Life Saver after she uses it. When the student has used all her Life Savers, she must try to answer questions without assistance.
3. Call on one student from each team in turn. Have the student sit near the overhead projector while you display a 75 dolphin dollar question. Read the question and allow the student time to respond or use one of her Life Savers.
4. If a question is missed, the team stays at that dollar amount and continues trying more difficult questions for the same quantity of dolphin dollars.
5. The first team to reach 1,000 dolphin dollars wins.

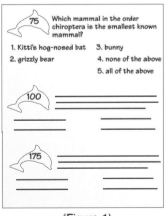

75 Which mammal in the order chiroptera is the smallest known mammal?
1. Kitti's hog-nosed bat   3. bunny
2. grizzly bear   4. none of the above
    5. all of the above

©The Education Center, Inc.

(Figure 1)

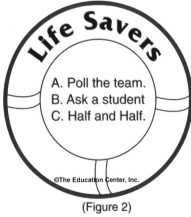

Life Savers

A. Poll the team.
B. Ask a student
C. Half and Half.

(Figure 2)

Dolphin Dollars	Team A	Team B
1000 dolphin dollars		
500 dolphin dollars		
250 dolphin dollars		
175 dolphin dollars		
100 dolphin dollars		
75 dolphin dollars		

(Figure 3)

⑤

The Nuances of Nesting
(Experiment, Simulation)

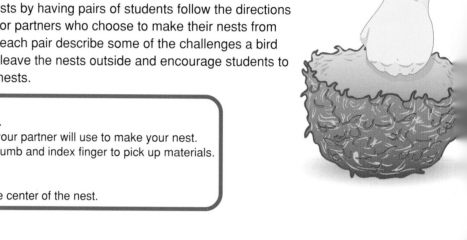

Ever wonder what goes into making a bird's nest? Let your students try their hands at nest building with this simulation activity. Explain to students that not all birds build nests. Of those that do, most make their nests bowl shaped. Further explain that birds build nests in two steps that happen at the same time. A bird collects its materials and then sits in the center of the nest, turning in a circular motion, then pushing and shaping the materials into a nest. Some birds need special supplies for their nests, so they spend more time than others searching for and collecting them. (For example, a swallow searches puddles to find a certain kind of mud for its nest.) Birds' nests are usually made from natural materials such as mud, seed heads, needles and leaves, and twigs and sticks. Sometimes man-made materials such as string, aluminum foil, twine, paper, or tissue end up in a bird's nest.

Have your students build their own nests by having pairs of students follow the directions below. Allow pairs to work outside. Monitor partners who choose to make their nests from mud. When the nests are finished, have each pair describe some of the challenges a bird might face when building a nest. Finally, leave the nests outside and encourage students to observe if any birds choose to use their nests.

Directions for each pair:
Step 1: Collect the materials for your nest.
- Decide which types of materials you and your partner will use to make your nest.
- To simulate a bird's beak, use only your thumb and index finger to pick up materials.
Step 2: Form the nest.
- Form the materials into a nest shape.
- Use your fist as shown to form a cup in the center of the nest.

Wondrous Wings
(Research, Observation)

Introduce your students to the wonderful world of bird wings with the following activity. Explain to students that birds are the most successful flying animals because of the design of their wings. Further explain that though birds' wings all share the same feather pattern, the wings of each species vary in size and shape, depending on the bird's lifestyle. Make an enlarged transparency of the wing patterns shown. Display the transparency and discuss the different wing types and their uses with students. Ask students to predict which birds probably have which wing shape based on their knowledge of some common birds. (For example, pigeons probably have broad, rounded wings because they take off quickly.) Next, pair students and assign each pair a bird from the list below. Have the pair use resource materials to research its bird's wing shape and use. Have the pair write its information on a sheet of construction paper cut to resemble the wing type of its bird. Set aside time for each pair to share its research with the class. Display the wings on a bulletin board titled "Wondrous Wings."

broad, rounded wing
- good for short distances and speed
- can be easily moved to help steer
- found on birds who pursue prey or escape enemies over a short distance

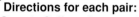

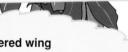

narrow, tapered wing
- good for flying long distances nonstop
- wing shape gives bird lift without too much *drag,* or air friction, that slows the bird down
- found on birds that are fast and powerful

long, pointed wing
- good for using less energy while flying
- birds soar using *thermals,* columns of warm, rising air, or they glide on *updrafts,* currents of air moving upward over cliffs and hills

finch	swift
woodpecker	peregrine falcon
grouse	gull
goose	buzzard
chaffinch	ring-necked pheasant
duck	

Oh, to Be a Tadpole!
(Research, Writing)

Did you know that most amphibians' eggs hatch into tadpoles and tadpolelike larvae? Let your students learn about the unique life cycle of some awesome amphibians with this activity. To begin, use the information shown to help you explain to students the differences between frogs and toads, and salamanders and newts. Next, have each student use encyclopedias or other resource materials to research the life cycle of one of these tadpole-producing amphibians. Then provide each child with the materials and a copy of the directions below to make a life cycle chart as shown. Finally, encourage students to compare and contrast the life cycles of these awesome amphibians.

Frogs and Toads
- Frogs and toads form the largest and most varied group of amphibians. They can live both in water and on land.
- Frogs have smoother skin than toads. They also have long back legs, webbed feet, and live in or near water.
- Toads have dry, wart-covered skin and little or no webbing on their feet. They prefer to live on land.

Salamanders and Newts
- Both look like lizards, but they don't have scaly skin.
- Salamanders are found near water. They live under rocks and in other dry places.
- Newts spend all of their lives in water.

Materials for each student:
1 legal-sized sheet of blank paper, ruler, one 12" x 18" sheet of construction paper, glue, scissors, and markers or crayons

Directions for each student:
1. Fold your sheet of blank paper in half lengthwise, leaving one side a half inch shorter than the other side (Figure 1).
2. Measure and mark six two-inch sections along the paper as shown. Then cut apart the sections and fold each tab up similar to a matchbook (Figure 2).
3. Write the steps of your amphibian's life cycle in order on the inside of each section; then add a picture of each life cycle step onto the front flap.
4. Glue each section in order and in a circular pattern onto a large sheet of construction paper. Draw arrows from each matchbook picture to indicate the order of the steps in the life cycle. (Figure 3)

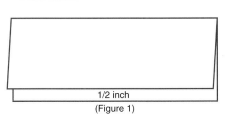

1/2 inch

(Figure 1)

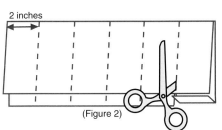

2 inches

(Figure 2)

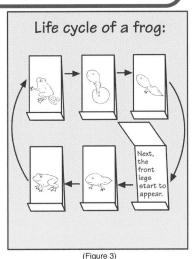

Life cycle of a frog:

Next, the front legs start to appear.

(Figure 3)

American Bullfrog

Ribbeting Research
(Research, Making a Glyph)

Your students will jump right into this fact-filled research project about frogs and toads! Explain to students that there are more than 3,900 different species of frogs and toads. This diverse group of amphibians can be found in a variety of shapes, sizes, and colors that help them adapt to different habitats including deserts, grasslands, and mountains. Have students research different frogs and toads and then use the information to make a special form of picture writing called a *glyph*. Assign each student a frog or toad from the list below and give him a copy of the reproducible on page 13. Have the student use resource materials to research his amphibian. Next, direct the student to follow the directions on page 13 to complete his glyph. Then provide each child with a nine-inch green paper plate, representing a lily pad. Instruct the student to glue his glyph onto the plate and label it with the name of his amphibian as shown. Then staple all the glyphs along with a glyph code on a bulletin board titled "Great Glyphs."

Frogs and Toads:
paradoxical frog	taitan toad
chorus frog	flying frog
American bullfrog	marsupial frog
arrow-poison frog	spadefoot toad
goliath frog	casque-headed frog

Reptile Real Estate
(Critical Thinking, Writing)

Here's a simple activity for helping students understand how cold-blooded vertebrates survive in a world of varying temperatures. Explain to students that reptiles are *cold-blooded,* which means that their body temperatures are the same as the temperature of their surroundings. For a reptile to survive, it must avoid extreme high and low temperatures. For that reason a reptile moves back and forth from sun to shade to keep from becoming too warm or too cool.

Have your students act as reptile real estate agents by finding sunny and shady areas on your playground or another outside location where reptiles might like to live. Pair students and give each pair an outdoor thermometer. Direct each pair to find either a sunny or a shady spot on the playground that might be suitable for a reptile and then place its thermometer in the chosen spot. Have the partners return to the classroom to describe their location and why it would be beneficial for a reptile and to predict the temperature of the location as you make a class chart as shown. After about 30 minutes, have the pairs return to their spots to gather the thermometers. Write the actual temperature of each area on the chart. Have each pair write a brief paragraph explaining the temperature of its location and why they think a reptile would live there. Instruct each pair to add a picture of a reptile living at its spot. Compile all of the paragraphs and pictures into a class book titled "Reptile Real Estate."

Names	Describe your spot.	Why would a reptile live there?	Predicted temperature	Actual temperature
Tim & Thad	A cool flat rock under a big tree.	It could stay cool in the afternoon.	56°	62°
Sue & Hope	On the curb near the drain.	It could stay warm and get water in the morning.	67°	70°
Ben & Melissa	A tree stump near the woods.	It could hide in the stump or rest on top.	64°	69°

"Sense-able" Snakes
(Experiment)

If you were a legless reptile with poor eyesight and hearing, how would you locate your prey? With the help of your tongue, of course! Use this experiment to help your students understand how snakes stake out their prey. Begin by making an enlarged transparency of the diagrams shown. Display the transparency and explain to students that a snake's tongue is used with a small organ in the roof of its mouth called *Jacobson's organ.* This organ has two sacs with many nerve endings that are sensitive to odors. A snake sticks out its tongue to pick up scents (Figure 1); then, as the tongue is returned to the snake's mouth, the scent particles enter the Jacobson's organ (Figure 2). Further explain that by using its tongue and the Jacobson's organ, a snake can follow the scent trail of its prey.

Have your students try to follow a scent trail like a snake by putting several drops of different scents—such as lemon, garlic, coffee, vanilla, or tuna fish—on five cotton balls. Place each cotton ball in a film canister. Next, put each of ten unscented cotton balls into a separate film canister. Number the scent canisters; then randomly place them around the classroom, making a trail. Have each student draw a map of the canisters, showing where they are placed in the classroom. Direct each student to walk the trail, smelling the contents of the canisters. Have him mark a trail of the scented canisters by coloring each one on his map. After every student has had a chance to go through the trail, have students reveal their maps and the numbers of the canisters they think were scented.

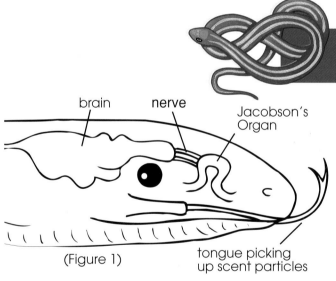

brain   nerve   Jacobson's Organ

(Figure 1)

tongue picking up scent particles

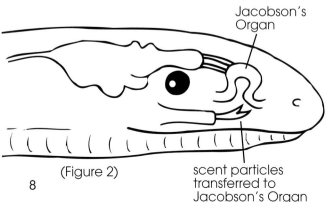

Jacobson's Organ

(Figure 2)

scent particles transferred to Jacobson's Organ

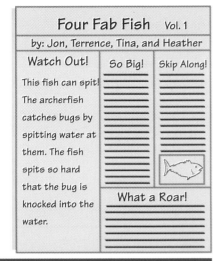

Four Fab Fish   Vol. 1

by: Jon, Terrence, Tina, and Heather

Watch Out!	So Big!	Skip Along!
This fish can spit! The archerfish catches bugs by spitting water at them. The fish spits so hard that the bug is knocked into the water.		
	What a Roar!	

What a Fish!
(Writing, Research)

Fascinate your students with this activity about some really far-out fish! Explain to students that fish come in all shapes, sizes, and colors. Further explain that some are so unique that they don't seem to belong to the fish class at all. Have each student use resource materials to research a fish from the list below. Direct the student to list unique characteristics of his fish. Next, group students and have each group member write a newspaper article about his assigned fish. Then have each group create a newspaper page using its articles. Encourage each group to add pictures of its fish along with a title to its newspaper. Finally, have each group read its newsworthy fish newspaper aloud to the class.

Far-Out Fish:
sargassum fish
lionfish
wrasse and blenny (two different fish)
porcupinefish
archerfish
whale shark
anableps
black swallower
flying hatchet fish
walking catfish
bristlemouth
mudskipper
electric eel
manta ray
spotted grouper
clownfish
sea horse

How Low Can They Go?
(Research, Critical Thinking)

Descend into the ocean depths to learn about some of the fish that live there. Explain to students that fish live in many different environments. Scientists classify these environments into two major groups: *saltwater* and *freshwater*. Further explain that more than half of all the fish species in the world live in the earth's main saltwater environment—the ocean. Of these fish, many can be found at different ocean depths. Share the information about the three main ocean depths with your students. Next, provide each student with the materials listed and a copy of the directions below. Have resource materials on hand for students' use. If desired, have each student write a brief paragraph summarizing her findings about the different fish species and their ocean homes.

Materials for each student:
one 12" x 18" sheet of medium blue construction paper, one 9" x 12" sheet each of dark blue and light blue construction paper, ruler, 2 lengths of blue plastic wrap, scissors, tape, glue, and markers or crayons

Directions:
1. Glue the light blue paper behind the large sheet of medium blue construction paper so that four inches of the light blue paper is visible at the top of the chart.
2. Glue the dark blue paper on top of the large sheet of medium blue construction paper so that seven inches of the medium blue paper is visible in the middle of the chart as shown.
3. Label each depth on the chart. Next, find several examples of fish species living in each of the three ocean depths. Draw a picture of each species in the correct depth; then add a sentence or two explaining the characteristics of some of the fish living in that water.
4. Cover the front of the chart with blue plastic wrap to represent water. Tape the plastic wrap to the back of the chart.

For many years scientists believed that sunlight was needed for fish to live in the deepest parts of the ocean. They now know that many fish species can live in the deepest and darkest parts of the ocean where there is very little sunlight. Scientists divide the ocean into three main levels according to the amount of sunlight that reaches each level. The *upper waters* (surface to 600 feet deep) receive the most sunlight. The fish that live in these waters are some of the largest and fastest-swimming fish such as marlin, swordfish, and a variety of sharks. Many different species of fish live in the *midwater depths* (600 to 3,000 feet deep). The water at this depth is dimly lit to completely dark. Most of the fish in the midwaters are small (measuring less than six inches long) and are a black, black-violet, or reddish brown color. Many fish living in the *depths,* or the deeper parts of the ocean (3,000 feet and deeper), have long, slim, pointed tails and large heads and eyes. These depths are dark and cold because they receive little or no sunlight.

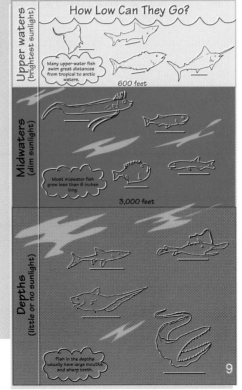

Name _____

Critical thinking

Collect a Class

Test your knowledge of the vertebrate classes with this "class-ic" game!

1. Fill in the answer box below by listing each animal shown under its correct class. Use encyclopedias, library books, or other reference materials to check your answer box.
2. Next, cut apart the animal cards. Shuffle and give each player five cards. Place the remaining cards facedown in a pile in the middle of the playing area.
3. Take turns asking the student on your left for either a reptile, fish, amphibian, mammal, or bird card. If that player doesn't have a card from that particular class, draw a card from the center pile.
4. Play continues until one person has all five cards from one class. Use the answer box to check your cards.

puffin	Komodo dragon	bush baby	salamander	stingray
tadpole	hedgehog	peacock	shark	gecko
gharial	sea horse	arrow-poison frog	platypus	owl
flamingo	spiny anteater	python	Gila monster	mudskipper
eel	giant tortoise	caecilian	dolphin	emu

Answer Box

mammals	fish	reptiles	amphibians	birds

©2000 The Education Center, Inc. • *Investigating Science • Animals* • TEC1731

Note to the teacher: Divide students into groups of three or five. Provide each group with one copy of this page and scissors. If desired, have each group color its animal cards and then glue them onto index cards for ease of handling.

10

What's in a Name?

Dr. H. Sapiens

Scientists call animals by their scientific names. That way no one gets confused!

Every living thing has a precise scientific name that identifies a single species and nothing else. For example, there are several species of jackal. To avoid confusing the species, scientists call each one by its scientific name such as *Canis aureus* (golden jackal).
Read each sentence below. Then use the coordinates to find the common name of each mammal.

	A	B	C	D	E	F	G	H	I	J
10	o			x				y		m
9		b			l		f			
8			g			q				
7									e	
6		t	h		s					
5			c				k			v
4						w				
3		n		d			p			r
2					i					
1	a									

1. The *Balaenoptera musculus* is the largest animal on Earth.
$$\overline{(B8)}\ \overline{(E9)}\ \overline{(A4)}\ \overline{(H6)}\quad \overline{(F3)}\ \overline{(D6)}\ \overline{(A1)}\ \overline{(E9)}\ \overline{(H6)}$$

2. The *Vulpes vulpes* catches rodents and other small prey by leaping in the air and landing on them.
$$\overline{(I2)}\ \overline{(H6)}\ \overline{(C2)}\quad \overline{(G8)}\ \overline{(A9)}\ \overline{(D10)}$$

3. The *Sarcophilus harrisii* eats every part of its prey.
$$\overline{(B6)}\ \overline{(A1)}\ \overline{(E5)}\ \overline{(J7)}\ \overline{(A1)}\ \overline{(B3)}\ \overline{(E1)}\ \overline{(A1)}\ \overline{(B3)}\quad \overline{(C2)}\ \overline{(H6)}\ \overline{(I4)}\ \overline{(E1)}\ \overline{(E9)}$$

4. The *Rangifer tarandus* is the only deer species in which both males and females have antlers.
$$\overline{(I2)}\ \overline{(H6)}\ \overline{(E1)}\ \overline{(B3)}\ \overline{(C2)}\ \overline{(H6)}\ \overline{(I2)}$$

5. Many *Sciurus carolinensis* hibernate during the fall and winter.
$$\overline{(C7)}\ \overline{(I2)}\ \overline{(A1)}\ \overline{(H9)}\quad \overline{(E5)}\ \overline{(F7)}\ \overline{(A4)}\ \overline{(E1)}\ \overline{(I2)}\ \overline{(I2)}\ \overline{(H6)}\ \overline{(E9)}$$

6. The *Ursus arctos* sometimes stands on its hind legs for a better view or to warn enemies.
$$\overline{(B8)}\ \overline{(I2)}\ \overline{(A9)}\ \overline{(F3)}\ \overline{(B3)}\quad \overline{(B8)}\ \overline{(H6)}\ \overline{(A1)}\ \overline{(I2)}$$

7. Though it is a different color, a *Panthera pardus* is actually a leopard.
$$\overline{(B8)}\ \overline{(E9)}\ \overline{(A1)}\ \overline{(B5)}\ \overline{(G4)}\quad \overline{(G2)}\ \overline{(A1)}\ \overline{(B3)}\ \overline{(B6)}\ \overline{(D6)}\ \overline{(H6)}\ \overline{(I2)}$$

8. The *Loxodonta africana* is the largest land animal and can weigh up to 6.6 tons.
$$\overline{(G4)}\ \overline{(E1)}\ \overline{(E9)}\ \overline{(E9)}\ \overline{(H6)}\ \overline{(I2)}\quad \overline{(F3)}\ \overline{(D6)}\ \overline{(A1)}\ \overline{(E9)}\ \overline{(H6)}$$

9. The species *Orcinus orca* often travels through the ocean in groups called pods.
$$\overline{(A1)}\ \overline{(G8)}\ \overline{(I2)}\ \overline{(E1)}\ \overline{(B5)}\ \overline{(A1)}\ \overline{(B3)}\quad \overline{(H6)}\ \overline{(E9)}\ \overline{(H6)}\ \overline{(G2)}\ \overline{(D6)}\ \overline{(A1)}\ \overline{(B3)}\ \overline{(B6)}$$

10. In the spring and summer the *Lepus americanus* has a brownish gray coat, but in the winter its coat turns white.
$$\overline{(E5)}\ \overline{(B3)}\ \overline{(A9)}\ \overline{(F3)}\ \overline{(E5)}\ \overline{(D6)}\ \overline{(A9)}\ \overline{(H6)}\quad \overline{(D6)}\ \overline{(A1)}\ \overline{(I2)}\ \overline{(H6)}$$

On the Move

Every spring, flocks of birds fly north, where they nest and raise their young. At the end of the summer, the birds *migrate,* or travel, south, where the weather is warmer. Many birds have flown along the same migration routes for thousands of years. Find out about these fabulous fliers by following the directions below.

Directions: Trace each migration route on the map in a different color. Next, color the corresponding number on the color key. Then use the map to help you answer the questions below.

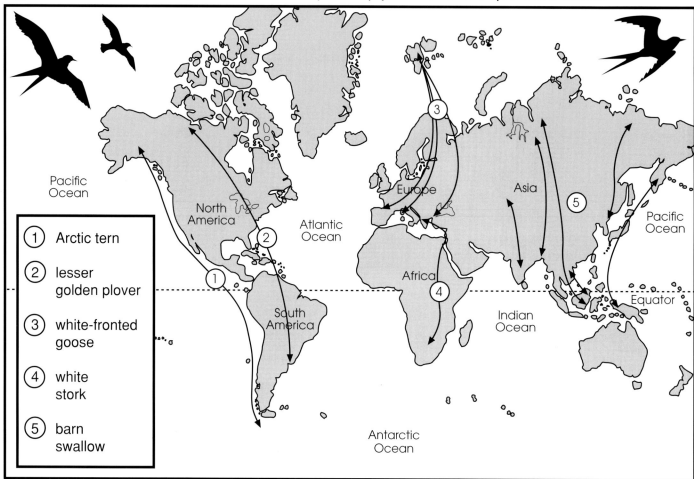

1. Which bird on the map flies the farthest? _____

2. Are there any birds that fly from North America to Europe? _____

3. Which bird flies to Europe? _____

4. Only one bird flies to islands on the map. Which bird is it?_____

5. Which bird(s) flies across the equator? _____

   _____

6. Which bird flies from North America to South America? _____

7. Which bird begins at the most northern spot on the map? _____

8. How many birds fly from north to south and then back again? _____

Great Glyphs

Research your assigned amphibian; then cut out the frog below. Use the glyph code to help you color the frog cutout so it shows information about your frog or toad.

Size: color the body
large—gray
medium—green
small—orange

Favorite food: color the head
eats insects—pink dots
eats fish—light blue dots
eats other animals—light green dots

Habitat: color the legs
lives in the rain forest—black stripes
lives in swamps/marshes—red and black stripes
lives mainly in water—blue stripes
lives in the desert or the mountains—brown stripes

Defense against enemies: color the mouth
changes colors—red
uses camouflage—purple
stings or poisons—green
hides—yellow

Movement: color the feet
takes long jumps—purple squiggles
crawls—blue squiggles
takes short jumps—orange squiggles
swims—blue squiggles

Type of amphibian: color the eyes
toad—red
frog—blue

Note to the teacher: Use with "Ribbeting Research" on page 7.

Snake Sssurvey

Some people are afraid of and dislike snakes, often because snakes are misunderstood. Find out how ten people feel about snakes by having them take the opinion poll below. See if their feelings change after they learn more about these reptiles.

Name of each person polled	How do you feel about snakes?	Do snakes seem strange and dangerous to you?	Did you know that not all snakes are poisonous?	Did you know that some snakes help to control rodents and other pests and that snake venom is used in medical and biological research?	Did you know that most snakes are harmless to people?	Now do you feel differently about snakes?
1.	☐ like ☐ dislike	☐ yes ☐ no	☐ yes ☐ no	☐ yes ☐ no	☐ yes ☐ no	☐ yes ☐ no
2.	☐ like ☐ dislike	☐ yes ☐ no	☐ yes ☐ no	☐ yes ☐ no	☐ yes ☐ no	☐ yes ☐ no
3.	☐ like ☐ dislike	☐ yes ☐ no	☐ yes ☐ no	☐ yes ☐ no	☐ yes ☐ no	☐ yes ☐ no
4.	☐ like ☐ dislike	☐ yes ☐ no	☐ yes ☐ no	☐ yes ☐ no	☐ yes ☐ no	☐ yes ☐ no
5.	☐ like ☐ dislike	☐ yes ☐ no	☐ yes ☐ no	☐ yes ☐ no	☐ yes ☐ no	☐ yes ☐ no
6.	☐ like ☐ dislike	☐ yes ☐ no	☐ yes ☐ no	☐ yes ☐ no	☐ yes ☐ no	☐ yes ☐ no
7.	☐ like ☐ dislike	☐ yes ☐ no	☐ yes ☐ no	☐ yes ☐ no	☐ yes ☐ no	☐ yes ☐ no
8.	☐ like ☐ dislike	☐ yes ☐ no	☐ yes ☐ no	☐ yes ☐ no	☐ yes ☐ no	☐ yes ☐ no
9.	☐ like ☐ dislike	☐ yes ☐ no	☐ yes ☐ no	☐ yes ☐ no	☐ yes ☐ no	☐ yes ☐ no
10.	☐ like ☐ dislike	☐ yes ☐ no	☐ yes ☐ no	☐ yes ☐ no	☐ yes ☐ no	☐ yes ☐ no

Bonus Box: Tally the totals of each column. Use your results to make a bar graph on the back of this page. What conclusions can you draw based on your graph?

Name_____

Class Portraits

There are three main groups of fish: bony fish, cartilaginous fish, and jawless fish. Draw pictures of each type of fish indicated in the picture frames below. Then write a brief description of the characteristics of each group of fish on the lines provided. Use encyclopedias, library books, and other reference materials to help you.

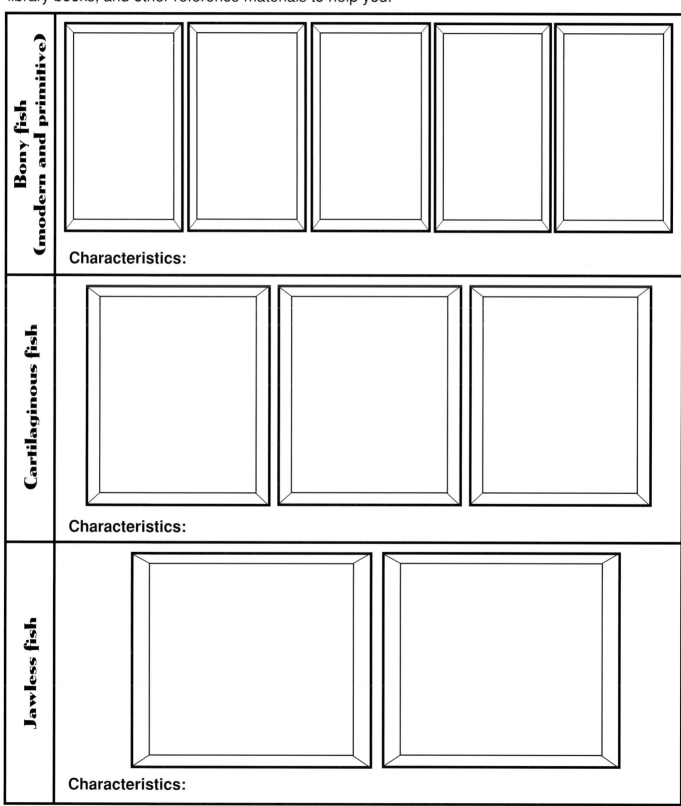

Bony fish (modern and primitive)

Characteristics:

Cartilaginous fish

Characteristics:

Jawless fish

Characteristics:

Invertebrates

Help your junior zoologists develop a soft spot for the spineless members of the animal kingdom with these activities, which are strong on fun!

Background for the Teacher

- *Invertebrates* are animals without backbone
- Invertebrates are divided into large groups called *phyla*.
- The major phyla of invertebrates are *Porifer Coelenterates, Platyhelminthes, Nematoda, Annelida, Echinodermata, Mollusca,* and *Arthropoda.*
- Instead of backbones, invertebrates have tough skin, strong shells, or hard, armorlike coverings called *exoskeletons* to support their bodies.
- More than 90 percent of the world's animals are invertebrates.
- More than three-fourths of all animals belong to the invertebrate phylum of arthropods. The largest class of arthropods is insects.

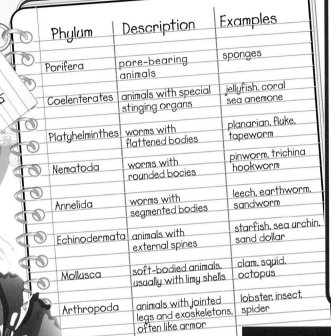

Phylum	Description	Examples
Porifera	pore-bearing animals	sponges
Coelenterates	animals with special stinging organs	jellyfish, coral sea anemone
Platyhelminthes	worms with flattened bodies	planarian, fluke, tapeworm
Nematoda	worms with rounded bodies	pinworm, trichina hookworm
Annelida	worms with segmented bodies	leech, earthworm, sandworm
Echinodermata	animals with external spines	starfish, sea urchin, sand dollar
Mollusca	soft-bodied animals, usually with limy shells	clam, squid, octopus
Arthropoda	animals with jointed legs and exoskeletons, often like armor	lobster, insect, spider

Nematoda

Porifera

worms with segmented bodies

earthworm

Ring Around the Invertebrates
(Vocabulary)

Have your students conversing like true "invertebrate-ologists" with this activity, which characterizes the eight major groups of invertebrates. Give each child eight index cards with holes punched in the upper left corners. Have the student copy a different phylum from the list above on the front of each card and its description on the back. Direct students to use reference books to help them add sample illustrations of the animals to the backs of the cards. Then give each child a metal ring for holding his cards together. Suggest that students clip the cards to their science notebooks to use as a quick reference tool.

Incredible Invertebrates Booklist

Invertebrate Zoology (Real Kids/Real Science Books series) by Ellen Doris (Thames and Hudson Inc., 1993)
Simple Animals (Encyclopedia of the Animal World series) by John Stidworthy (Facts on File, Inc.; 1990)
Small Sea Creatures: The Sea (Discovery Library of the Sea series) by Jason Cooper (The Rourke Book Company, Inc.; 1992)
Sorting Out Worms and Other Invertebrates: Everything You Want to Know About Insects, Corals, Mollusks, Sponges, and More! (Sorting Out series) by Samuel G. Woods (Blackbirch Marketing, 1999)
Wings, Stings and Wriggly Things (SuperSmarts series) by Martin Jenkins (Candlewick Press, 1998)

Mollusks on the Menu
(Descriptive Writing)

Make students' mouths water with a menu-writing activity that can tempt their taste buds! Review with students that mollusks are soft-bodied animals that are used mainly for food. Next, help students brainstorm a list of common mollusks (snail, slug, mussel, oyster, clam, scallop, octopus, squid). Then give each child a sheet of white construction paper and crayons or markers. Have her use the materials to create a menu for an imaginary restaurant called The Hard Shell Cafe. Explain that this restaurant serves only entrees prepared from mollusks, such as New England clam chowder and broiled scallops. On her menu, have the student include the names of several different entrees and a description and illustration of each one. Display the completed menus on a bulletin board titled "Now Serving…Menus Full of Mollusks!" If desired, follow up with a tasting party by having parents provide toothpicked samples of several different mollusks. Bon appétit!

Appetizers

Oysters Rockefeller

Oysters on the Half Shell

New England Clam Chowder

Entrees

Broiled Scallops

Snails

Fried Squid

Fried Oysters & Scallops

- A jellyfish is about 95 percent water.
- Jellyfish are older than dinosaurs.
- Jellyfish live in oceans all over the world. Some even live in lakes.
- An adult jellyfish's body is called a *medusa* because it resembles a similar character from Greek mythology.
- Some people eat jellyfish as a delicacy.
- The most dangerous jellyfish is Australia's box jelly. Its toxin is more deadly than a cobra's venom.

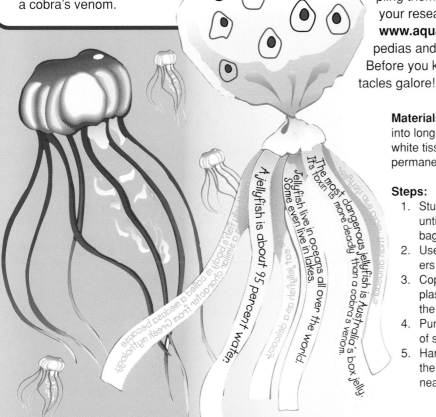

Jellyfish Jargon
(Research)

Interest your students in the soft-bodied members of the coelenterate phylum with a research activity that really jells! First, create a model of a jellyfish by following the steps below. Then challenge your students to add more tentacles to the model by researching other interesting jellyfish facts, writing them on the long plastic strips, and stapling them to the bottom of the model. Suggest that your researchers use Web sites such as **www.aqua.org/animals/species/jellies** plus encyclopedias and other reference books to find information. Before you know it, the class's jelly friend will have tentacles galore!

Materials: scissors; 2 white plastic garbage bags, 1 cut into long strips about 1" wide and stored in a container; white tissue paper; 1 twist-tie; tape (optional); stapler; permanent markers; hole puncher; string or yarn

Steps:
1. Stuff the white plastic garbage bag with tissue paper until it is shaped like a bell. If necessary, tape the bag's corners to give them a rounded look.
2. Use a twist-tie to close the bag's opening. Use markers to decorate the outside of the bag as shown.
3. Copy one or more of the facts above onto different plastic strips. Staple the strips to the bottom edge of the bag to represent tentacles.
4. Punch a hole in the top center of the bag. Tie a length of string through the hole.
5. Hang the jellyfish in a corner of the classroom with the container of strips and the permanent markers nearby.

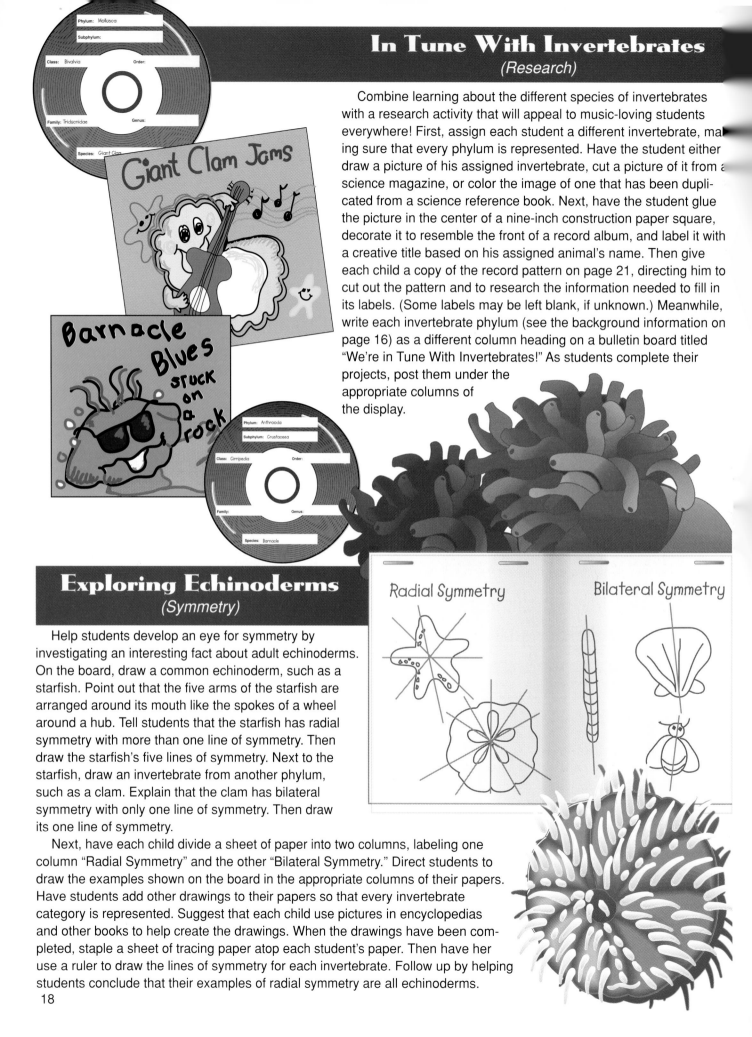

Phylum: Mollusca
Subphylum:
Class: Bivalvia   **Order:**
Family: Tridacnidae   **Genus:**
Species: Giant Clam

Giant Clam Jams

Barnacle Blues stuck on a rock

Phylum: Anthropoda
Subphylum: Crustacea
Class: Cirripedia   **Order:**
Family: **Genus:**
Species: Barnacle

In Tune With Invertebrates
(Research)

Combine learning about the different species of invertebrates with a research activity that will appeal to music-loving students everywhere! First, assign each student a different invertebrate, making sure that every phylum is represented. Have the student either draw a picture of his assigned invertebrate, cut a picture of it from a science magazine, or color the image of one that has been duplicated from a science reference book. Next, have the student glue the picture in the center of a nine-inch construction paper square, decorate it to resemble the front of a record album, and label it with a creative title based on his assigned animal's name. Then give each child a copy of the record pattern on page 21, directing him to cut out the pattern and to research the information needed to fill in its labels. (Some labels may be left blank, if unknown.) Meanwhile, write each invertebrate phylum (see the background information on page 16) as a different column heading on a bulletin board titled "We're in Tune With Invertebrates!" As students complete their projects, post them under the appropriate columns of the display.

Exploring Echinoderms
(Symmetry)

Help students develop an eye for symmetry by investigating an interesting fact about adult echinoderms. On the board, draw a common echinoderm, such as a starfish. Point out that the five arms of the starfish are arranged around its mouth like the spokes of a wheel around a hub. Tell students that the starfish has radial symmetry with more than one line of symmetry. Then draw the starfish's five lines of symmetry. Next to the starfish, draw an invertebrate from another phylum, such as a clam. Explain that the clam has bilateral symmetry with only one line of symmetry. Then draw its one line of symmetry.

Radial Symmetry   Bilateral Symmetry

Next, have each child divide a sheet of paper into two columns, labeling one column "Radial Symmetry" and the other "Bilateral Symmetry." Direct students to draw the examples shown on the board in the appropriate columns of their papers. Have students add other drawings to their papers so that every invertebrate category is represented. Suggest that each child use pictures in encyclopedias and other books to help create the drawings. When the drawings have been completed, staple a sheet of tracing paper atop each student's paper. Then have her use a ruler to draw the lines of symmetry for each invertebrate. Follow up by helping students conclude that their examples of radial symmetry are all echinoderms.

About how long is the worm you are observing? *(Answers will vary.)*

Does the worm have eyes? *(No.)* Ears? *(No.)*

Does the worm have legs or arms? *(No.)*

Does the worm have a mouth? *(Yes.)*

How does the worm react when you gently touch it with the eraser end of a pencil? *(It moves away from the eraser.)*

How does the earthworm use its *setae,* or bristles? *(To move.)*

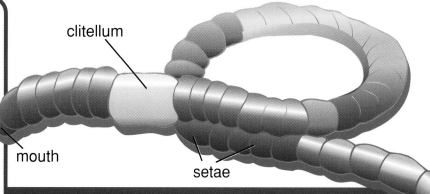

clitellum

mouth

setae

A Worm's World
(Observation)

Adopt earthworms as wriggly classroom pets to help your students learn more about the annelids, the most highly developed group of worms. Using a gardening trowel, collect earthworms, soil, leaves, and other organic material from a moist area outside. Store the contents in a glass jar that has a lid with holes. Place the jar at a center along with the questions above. Introduce the center to students by reviewing with them the parts of an earthworm (see the illustration). Then, as students visit the center, have them use their observation skills to answer the questions posted. When all students have visited the center, discuss the questions and answers together as a class. Afterward, release the worms outside in an area of moist soil.

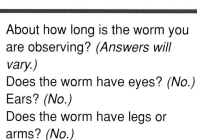

Painting With Porifera
(Art)

Have a "hole" lot of fun by having students use sponges to create scenes of this pore-bearing animal's natural habitat. Gather pictures that show where sponges live. Purchase several bath sponges and cut them into different-sized pieces. Arrange several plastic plates on a newspaper-covered surface; then pour a different color of tempera paint onto each plate. Place three sponge pieces next to each plate. Next, show students the pictures you have gathered. Explain that sponges live in either oceans or bodies of fresh water, such as rivers and lakes. Also explain that the skeletons of certain sponges are soft and can absorb large amounts of water. Then give each child a sheet of blue construction paper on which to sponge-paint an underwater scene showing where sponges live. Display the resulting scenes on a bulletin board titled "Porifera's Home, Sweet Home."

As a variation, have students sponge-paint attractive borders around the edges of recycled paper. When the papers have dried, have students tie the sheets together in bundles with ribbon and give them as gifts of stationery to friends and family members.

Armored Arthropods
(Critical Thinking, Art, Writing)

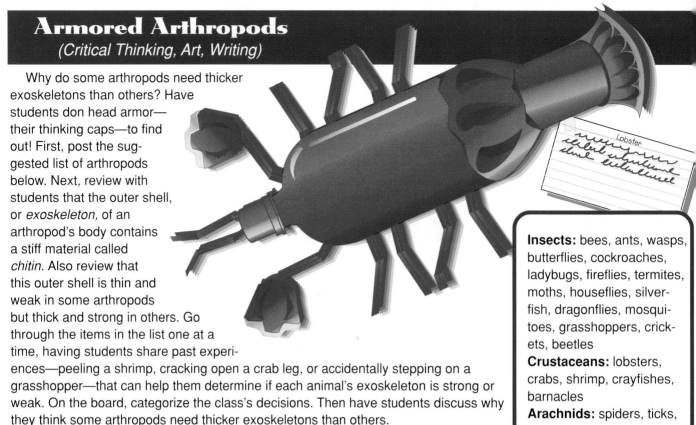

Why do some arthropods need thicker exoskeletons than others? Have students don head armor—their thinking caps—to find out! First, post the suggested list of arthropods below. Next, review with students that the outer shell, or *exoskeleton,* of an arthropod's body contains a stiff material called *chitin.* Also review that this outer shell is thin and weak in some arthropods but thick and strong in others. Go through the items in the list one at a time, having students share past experiences—peeling a shrimp, cracking open a crab leg, or accidentally stepping on a grasshopper—that can help them determine if each animal's exoskeleton is strong or weak. On the board, categorize the class's decisions. Then have students discuss why they think some arthropods need thicker exoskeletons than others.

Follow up by having students bring in common recyclable materials to make creative models of arthropods. Expect to see spray-painted creations made of taped-together two-liter bottles, egg cartons, paper towel rolls, foil, etc. Then challenge each student to write a short paragraph describing his arthropod's body structure on an index card and tape it to his model. Display the resulting army of arthropods in your school's media center for interested onlookers to view.

Insects: bees, ants, wasps, butterflies, cockroaches, ladybugs, fireflies, termites, moths, houseflies, silverfish, dragonflies, mosquitoes, grasshoppers, crickets, beetles
Crustaceans: lobsters, crabs, shrimp, crayfishes, barnacles
Arachnids: spiders, ticks, scorpions
Chilopods: centipedes
Diplopods: millipedes

Encyclopedia Invertebrata
(Booklet-Making Review)

Make sure you've covered invertebrates from *A* to *Z* with a culminating project that produces a mini-library of picture encyclopedias. Give each student the materials listed. Then guide him through the steps below to make a class set of resources that future zoologists can peruse in your school's media center.

Materials: 9" x 12" sheet of colorful construction paper, 13 sheets of loose-leaf paper cut in half, stapler, crayons or markers

Steps:
1. Fold the construction paper in half.
2. Place the loose-leaf sheets inside the folded paper and staple as shown.
3. Label each loose-leaf page with a different letter of the alphabet.
4. On each booklet page, write the name of a specific invertebrate phylum, class, species, etc., that begins with the letter on that page.
5. Write a description for each invertebrate. If possible, include an illustration.
6. Decorate your booklet's cover.

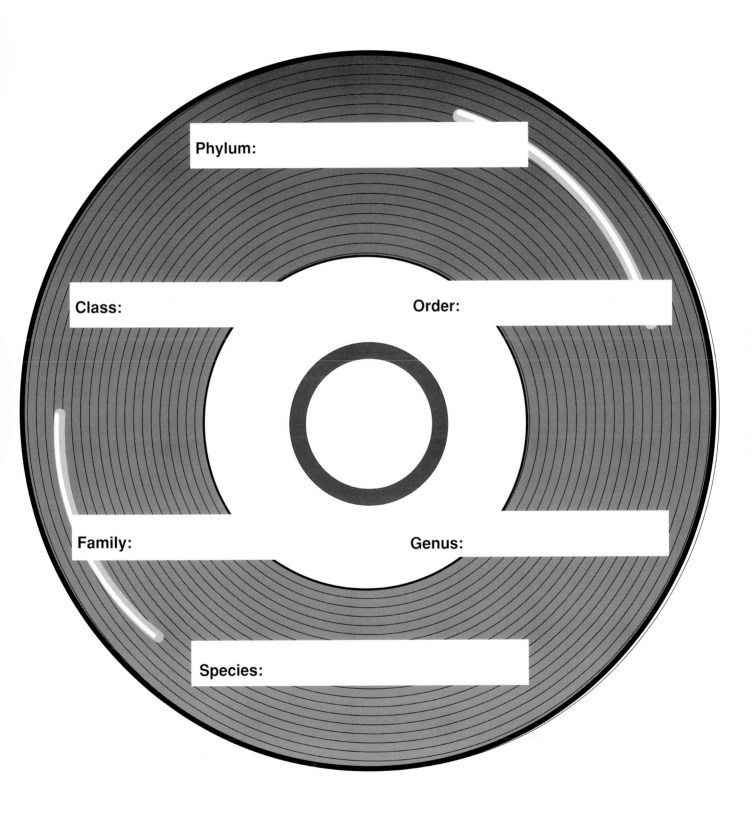

Phylum:

Class:

Order:

Family:

Genus:

Species:

Invertebrates in Action

Stephen Spineberg, a famous film director, is having auditions for parts in *The Empire Strikes Backless,* the upcoming sequel to his successful movie *Spine Wars.* Stephen wants to fill each role with the actor whose attributes best match those of the character being cast.

Part 1: Read the descriptions below. Decide which actor is best suited for each role. Write his or her name on the line provided.

Actors

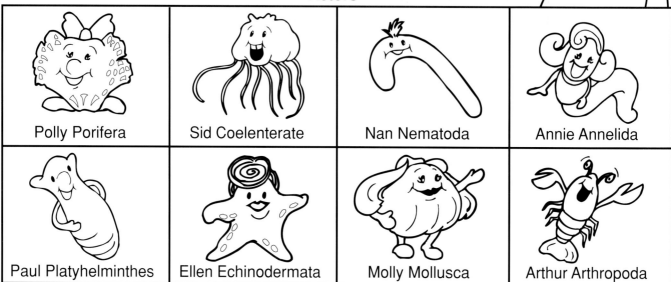

| Polly Porifera | Sid Coelenterate | Nan Nematoda | Annie Annelida |
| Paul Platyhelminthes | Ellen Echinodermata | Molly Mollusca | Arthur Arthropoda |

Role 1 _____ .
This role must be played by an animal that has an external spine and radial symmetry.

Role 2 _____ .
This role must be played by a soft-bodied animal that has a limy shell.

Role 3 _____ .
This role must be played by an animal that has jointed legs and an exoskeleton of chitin.

Role 4 _____ .
This role must be played by a worm that has a segmented body.

Role 5 _____ .
This role must be played by a worm that has a flattened body.

Role 6 _____ .
This role must be played by a sponge, or pore-bearing animal.

Role 7 _____ .
This role must be played by an animal that lives in the ocean and has a special stinging organ called a nematocyst.

Role 8 _____ .
This role must be played by a roundworm, preferably a pinworm or a hookworm.

Part 2: On the back of this page or on another sheet of paper, write the dialogue for a scene you'd like to include in Stephen Spineberg's movie. Include at least three actors listed above.

No-Bones-About-It Math

Directions: Solve each problem below to get a value for each letter of the alphabet. Use the products to answer the trivia questions about invertebrates listed below.

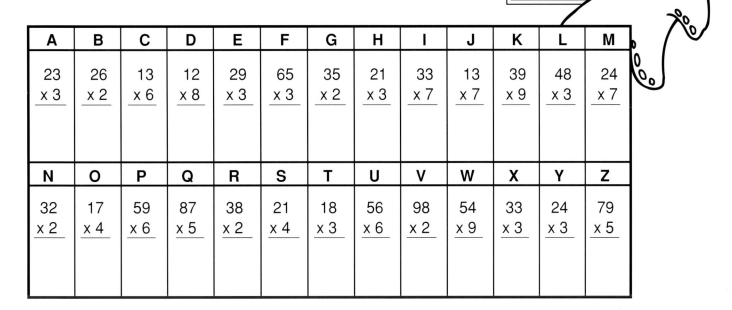

A	B	C	D	E	F	G	H	I	J	K	L	M
23 x 3	26 x 2	13 x 6	12 x 8	29 x 3	65 x 3	35 x 2	21 x 3	33 x 7	13 x 7	39 x 9	48 x 3	24 x 7

N	O	P	Q	R	S	T	U	V	W	X	Y	Z
32 x 2	17 x 4	59 x 6	87 x 5	38 x 2	21 x 4	18 x 3	56 x 6	98 x 2	54 x 9	33 x 3	24 x 3	79 x 5

1. The number of known invertebrate species is more than __ __ __   __ __ __ __ __ __ __.
   68 64 87   168 231 144 144 231 68 64

2. This very aggressive meat-eating arthropod carries its young on its back. __ __   __ __ __ __ __ __
   84 78   68 76 354 231 68 64

3. This mollusk releases millions of eggs into the water each year but does nothing to care for any offspring that survive. __ __   __ __
   78 144   69 168

4. This coelenterate has a glow caused by tiny plantlike bacteria living in it. This glow helps the animal attract its prey. __ __ __ __   __ __ __ __ __
   91 87 144 144   72 195 231 84 63

5. This member of the porifera phylum is so indestructible that it can rebuild body parts that are broken off. __ __ __ __ __ __
   84 354 68 64 70 87

6. The largest of these animals can grow to be many feet or meters long. __ __ __ __ __
   486 68 76 168 84

7. If this echinoderm loses an arm during an attack, it can grow a new one. __ __   __ __ __ __ __ __
   84 54   69 76 195 231 84 63

8. One end of this hollow, cylinder-shaped animal is attached to the bottom of the sea, while its mouth and tentacles are at the other end. __ __ __   __ __ __ __ __ __ __
   84 87 69   69 64 87 168 68 64 87

9. Echinoderms have rows of special body parts called __ __ __ __   __ __ __ __, which can form suction disks to grip hard surfaces.
   54 336 52 87   195 87 87 54

10. This animal can be "right-handed" or "left-handed," depending on which side of its body has the larger claw. __ __   __ __ __ __ __
    144 68   52 84 54 87 76

Insects

Use this collection of creepy-crawly activities to introduce your students to the fascinating world of insects.

Background for the Teacher

- Insects have existed on the earth for at least 400 million years. They live in water and in polar, desert, and tropical regions.
- Insects have three main body parts: the *head,* the *thorax,* and the *abdomen.*
- The head consists of mouthparts, eyes, and antennae.
- Six legs and wings (if present) are attached to the insect's midsection, the thorax.
- The abdomen consists of digestive and reproductive organs and, in some insects, a pair of feelers called *cerci.*
- Insects have *exoskeletons* (external skeletons), which are lighter and stronger than bone.
- Most adult insects have two large compound eyes consisting of many six-sided lenses that work together to form a complete picture. Insects may also have *ocelli* (three simple eyes) between the two compound eyes. Ocelli distinguish between light and dark.
- Insects may fly, jump, run away, sting, bite, produce a terrible smell, or hide in defense.
- Insects feed on plants and animals and are also food for plants and animals. They also pollinate crops, provide honey and other products, and prey on other insects.
- Some insects are pests to people—biting, spreading diseases, damaging property, and destroying crops.
- Chemical control, biological control, and other methods are used to control insects.

Presto Change-o!
(Research, Completing a Diagram)

Use this activity to introduce your students to the unique phenomenon called *metamorphosis.* Begin by explaining that insects experience one of two types of metamorphosis: *complete* or *incomplete.* Complete metamorphosis has four stages: *egg, larva, pupa,* and *adult.* Incomplete metamorphosis has three stages: *egg, nymph* (larva), and *adult.* Further explain that as the insect grows, *molting* also occurs. During molting, the exoskeleton splits open, the insect wriggles out, and its new exoskeleton unfolds and hardens around the insect.

Have your students investigate more about metamorphosis with the following research activity. Divide your students into small groups. Provide each group with access to reference books on insects. Then have each group research to find one example of an insect that experiences complete metamorphosis and one insect that experiences incomplete metamorphosis. Also challenge each group to find out how many times each insect molts. Next, give each group one copy of page 29, two 9" x 12" sheets of colored construction paper, scissors, and glue. Then instruct the group to label and illustrate each stage of each insect's metamorphosis in the appropriate diagram on page 29. When the diagrams are complete, instruct the group to cut them out and mount each on a colored sheet of construction paper. Then have each group share its diagrams with the rest of the class. Display all the diagrams on a bulletin board titled "Wow! What a Change!"

Beautiful Bug Books!

Cicadas and Aphids: What They Have in Common (Animals in Order series) by Sara Swan Miller (Franklin Watts, Inc.; 1999)

The Cricket's Cage: A Chinese Folktale retold by Stefan Czernecki (Hyperion Books for Children, 1997)

Insect (Eyewitness Books) by Laurence Mound (Alfred A. Knopf, Inc.; 1990)

Insect Metamorphosis: From Egg to Adult by Ron and Nancy Goor (Atheneum, 1990)

Joyful Noise: Poems for Two Voices by Paul Fleischman (HarperCollins Publishers, Inc.; 1990)

Some Bugs Glow in the Dark (I Didn't Know That) by Claire Llewellyn (Copper Beech Books, 1997)

I Didn't Know That!
(Determining Fact or Fiction)

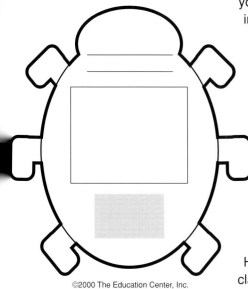

Amaze and astound your students by informing them that some insects glow in the dark, some can walk on water, and others taste with their feet. Then inform your students that they are going to work in pairs to research more interesting insect facts to use in creating a class insect fact or fiction book. Enlarge the insect pattern shown. Then give each pair two copies of the enlarged pattern, two rectangles of colored construction paper (cut to the size of the shaded box on the enlarged pattern), crayons, glue, and scissors. Assign each pair a different insect to research and supply the pairs with appropriate reference materials. Next, instruct each pair to research one amazing fact about the assigned insect. Then direct the pair to create one fictitious statement about the insect so that it appears to be fact. Direct the pair to write the fact at the top of one of the enlarged patterns, illustrate it in the center of the pattern, write "Fact" in the shaded box at the bottom of the pattern, and then cut out the pattern. Have the pair repeat the process for the fictitious statement, using the second pattern and writing "Fiction" in the shaded box. Next, instruct the pair to cover each shaded box with an answer flap by gluing one edge of each small construction paper rectangle to the top of each shaded box as shown. Have each pair read aloud its fact and fiction statements and try to stump the class. After each pair has shared its statements, compile all the patterns into one booklet titled "Amazing Insects: Fact or Fiction?"

©2000 The Education Center, Inc.

Jug Bug Mask
(Insect Anatomy, Making a Model)

Introduce students to the facial features of insects with these creative insect masks. Explain that insect heads have three main parts: the mouthparts, eyes, and antennae. Point out that an insect's mouth is adapted to its diet. Chewing insects, such as grasshoppers and termites, have powerful jaws called *mandibles.* Insects such as mosquitoes and bedbugs have structures that pierce food and suck juices or blood. Honeybees, which drink nectar and chew wax to build hives, have chewing and sucking structures. Butterflies have a tubelike structure, a *proboscis* that sucks liquids and coils up when not in use. After sharing this information, provide students with the materials listed and guide them through the steps below to create the masks.

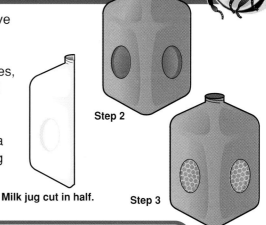

Milk jug cut in half.

Step 2

Step 3

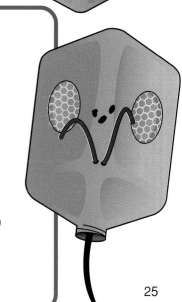

Materials for each student: 1 clean gallon milk jug cut in half vertically as shown; 1 black pipe cleaner; red and brown poster paint; paintbrush; glue; 3" x 6" piece of bubble wrap; tape; black permanent marker; 1 copy of the mouth patterns on page 30; newspaper; scissors

Steps:
1. Paint the outside of the jug brown. Set on newspaper to dry.
2. To create each compound eye, paint two red three-inch circles on the jug as shown. Then cut two three-inch circles from the bubble wrap.
3. Glue one bubble wrap circle on top of each painted circle as shown.
4. Use the marker to make three simple eye spots between the two compound eyes as shown.
5. Using scissors, carefully poke two small holes through the plastic between the two compound eyes. Fold the pipe cleaner in half and insert (from the back side of the mask) each end of the pipe cleaner through a hole. Secure with tape on the inside of the jug. Bend or curl the pipe cleaner ends to resemble antennae.
6. Choose a mouth pattern from page 30. Color it black and cut it out. Tape the mouthpart to the inside of the jug's spout as shown.

Incredible Insect Information

- An insect's body consists of three sections: the head, the thorax, and the abdomen.
- Insects take in air through holes (spiracles) along their bodies.
- Insects don't have veins or arteries, and their blood (which surrounds the inside parts of the insect's body) is greenish, yellowish, or colorless.
- The heart of an insect consists of a long tube that runs along its back.
- The digestive system of an insect is a tube that runs through the middle of the body.
- The muscular gizzard helps the insect grind up food.
- The nervous system consists of a brain located in the insect's head and two nerve cords that run side by side along the base of the thorax and abdomen.

Insects Inside and Out
(Insect Anatomy, Making a Model)

If insects were the size of people, they'd seem like aliens from outer space with their green blood, huge eyes, and airholes along the sides of their bodies. Use the following insect anatomy activity to help your students learn more about the amazing bodies of insects. In advance, create a transparency of "Incredible Insect Information" shown on this page. Then distribute to each student one copy of the insect diagram at the bottom of page 30. As you read aloud each incredible fact, have each student locate and label the corresponding section of the insect diagram. To assess your students' learning of the insect anatomy, have each student build an edible insect model. Provide students with the materials listed below. Then have each student follow the steps below as well as use his completed diagram (page 30) to build his model. After checking to see that each student has correctly completed his edible insect model, allow the students to dig in to their creations!

Materials for each student: 1/2 regular-sized Mounds® candy bar, six 2" lengths of black licorice, two 1" lengths of black licorice, decorating gel (blue, green, and red), paper towels

Steps:

1. Lay the Mounds® candy on a paper towel and form the three insect body sections—head, thorax, abdomen—by pinching the sides gently toward the center in two places. This represents a side view of the insect.
2. Use the two-inch lengths of licorice to position the insect's legs in the appropriate body section of the insect *(along the bottom of the thorax).*
3. Use the two one-inch licorice strips as antennae. Insert them into the appropriate body section of the insect *(top of the head).*
4. Use a lump of blue gel to mark the location of the brain *(center of the head).*
5. Squeeze a bumpy line of green gel onto the appropriate body sections of the insect to represent the insect's heart. *(The line should begin at the brain and run along the top of the thorax and abdomen.)*
6. Squeeze a bumpy line of red gel onto the appropriate body sections of the insect to represent the insect's digestive system. *(The line should begin at the brain and run along the middle of the thorax and abdomen.)*
7. Make two large red gel lumps on the digestive system gel line showing the location of the gizzard *(in the thorax just above the second leg)* and the stomach *(in the abdomen just above the hind leg).*
8. Squeeze a bumpy line of blue gel onto the appropriate body sections of the insect to represent the insect's nervous system. *(The line should begin at the brain and run along the bottom of the thorax and abdomen.)*

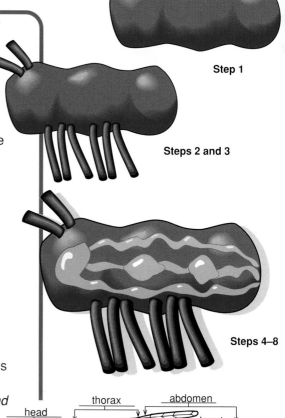

Step 1

Steps 2 and 3

Steps 4–8

Insects Right Under Your Nose
(Investigation, Research, Mapping)

The world around us is swarming with interesting insects. Introduce your students to the insect world by taking them on schoolyard field trips to map out insect habitats and observe insect life. Ahead of time, cover a bulletin board with light-colored paper and sketch a simple map of your school grounds. Involve students in illustrating the map with likely insect habitats such as trees, sidewalks, trash bins, playground equipment, etc. To begin the activity, divide the class into small groups and assign one area on the map to each group.

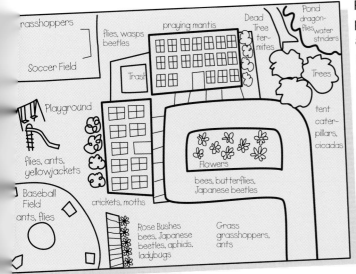

Provide each student with a copy of the observation form on page 31; then take each group outside to search its assigned area for insects. (Having an adult, such as a parent volunteer, accompany each group on its search is recommended.) Instruct each student to fill out his observation form for one of the insects found and observed by his group. Upon returning to the classroom, provide each group with an insect field guide and have the group members work together to attempt to identify the insects observed. Then have each group record the observed insects' names in the appropriate area of the map on the bulletin board. Repeat the activity for several days, rotating groups through the assigned areas. Compile the observation sheets into a class field guide, and donate it to your school library when your study of insects is complete. Your students will be amazed at how many insects live right under their noses!

Cricket Cabanas
(Making a Cricket Habitat, Observing)

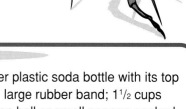

Most everyone is familiar with that unique chirping sound that fills the air in the early evening. Re-create that sound in your classroom by having your students build cricket cabanas to house a classroom of crickets. Providing food and shelter for crickets will offer students the opportunity to closely observe insect behavior. Ahead of time, gather the materials listed at the right as well as a class supply of crickets and a class supply of two-liter plastic soda bottles with the tops cut off. (Crickets can be purchased at most pet stores or through Carolina Biological Supply, 1-800-334-5551.)

Begin the activity by reading *The Cricket's Cage: A Chinese Folktale,* retold by Stefan Czernecki. Discuss the story and explain to students that, for centuries, the people of China kept pet crickets. Point out that the Chinese people enjoyed the cheerful chirping sounds and believed that crickets brought good luck. Then guide each student through the steps shown to create her own cricket cabana. Following your study of insects, release the crickets into a safe and appropriate habitat.

Materials for each student: 1 two-liter plastic soda bottle with its top cut off; 1 leg of a pair of panty hose; 1 large rubber band; 1$\frac{1}{2}$ cups potting soil; dry twig; small stone; cotton ball or small sponge soaked with water; apple slice, potato peelings, and/or lettuce; 1 cricket

Steps:
1. Pour the soil into the bottle and arrange the twig and stone on top.
2. Place fingertip-size food scraps and the damp cotton ball or sponge on the soil.
3. Gently place the cricket into the bottle and quickly cover the top with a section of panty hose. Secure the panty hose with a rubber band.
4. Wash hands after handling the crickets.
5. Observe the cricket daily and record in a science journal information about the cricket's anatomy, favorite foods, and behavior.

Most Valuable Insect Award!
(Research, Writing, Art)

Involve your students in building up the public image of beneficial insects with this unique activity combining research, persuasive writing, and art. Ahead of time, collect reference books on insects for students to share. Then supply each student with one five-inch poster board circle and crayons or markers. To begin, explain that many insects are a valuable natural resource, providing food for other animals, pollinating crops, and producing products such as honey, beeswax, silk, and shellac. Next, list on a sheet of chart paper the beneficial insects shown on this page. Assign each student one insect listed (more than one student will be assigned the same insect). Then direct the student to research the benefits of her assigned insect and its value to people. Inform the student that she's going to use the facts she's researched and the poster board circle to create a campaign button promoting her insect for the "Most Valuable Insect Award." Instruct the student to rewrite on the poster board circle the facts she's gathered in the form of a brief advertisement. Also direct the student to draw a picture of the insect on the button. When the buttons have been completed, have each student tell the class why her insect should win the award. Display the buttons for a few days. Then hold a classwide vote to determine which insect wins the award.

Vote Ladybug for Most Valuable Insect!

Ladybugs can eat as many as 100 pesky aphids in one day!

Beneficial Insects

lacewings	silkworms	honeybees	praying mantises
ladybugs	butterflies	moths	wasps

Pesky Insects
(Research, Art)

Challenge your students to dig up the *dirt* on pesky insects with this unique research activity. Ahead of time, list on the chalkboard the pesky insects shown below; then gather a supply of insect reference books. Begin the activity by pointing out that although some insects are beneficial, other insects are pests that spread disease and destroy property. Next, divide your students into pairs. Then write the following categories on the board: "We Destroy Crops" "We Destroy Forest, Fruit, and Shade Trees" "We Spread Disease," and "We Damage Houses and Other Property." Assign each pair a different pesky insect. Then instruct the pair to research its assigned insect to see in which categories the insect belongs. (Some insects may fall under more than one category.) Give each pair a piece of poster board and markers. Instruct each pair to create a Wanted poster for its insect. Tell the pair to include the following information on the poster: insect's name, a description of the insect, the damage/harm it causes, and the methods humans use to attempt to control the insect. After all the Wanted posters are complete, have each pair share its work with the class. Display all the posters on the wall outside your classroom under the heading "Pesky Insects and Their Dirty Deeds."

WANTED

Name: Colorado beetle

Description: Looks similar to a ladybug but is yellow with black stripes

Dirty Deed: Damages potato crops

Control Method: Insecticides

by Duncan and Troy

Pesky Insects

boll weevil	chinch bug	corn earworm	fire ant
gypsy moth	Japanese beetle	locust	flea
mosquito	Colorado beetle	termite	German cockroach
aphid	Hessian fly	silverfish	carpet beetle

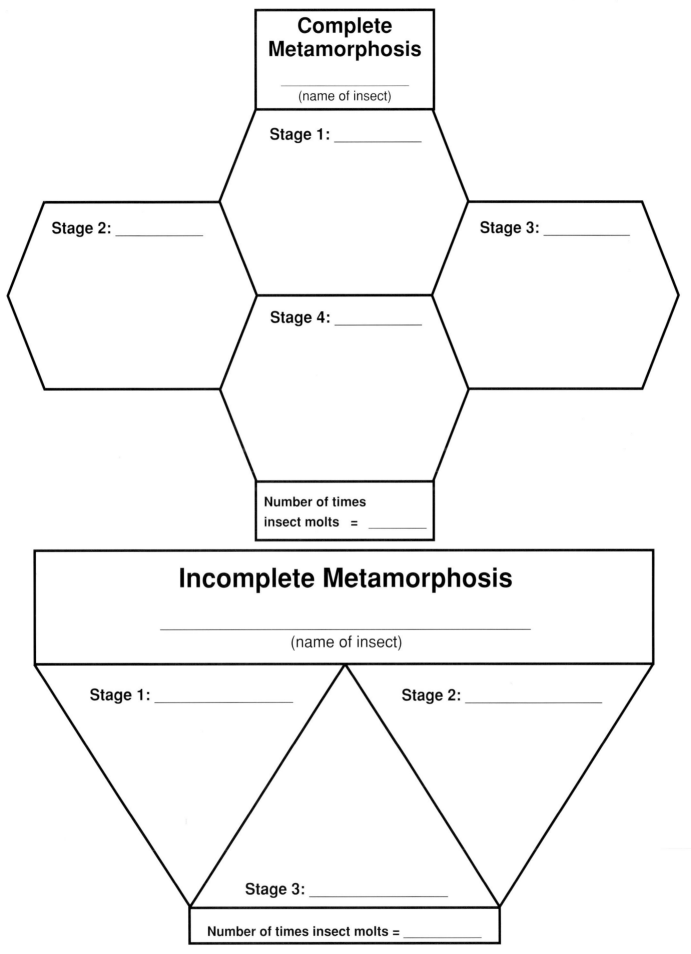

Complete Metamorphosis

_____
(name of insect)

Stage 1: _____

Stage 2: _____

Stage 3: _____

Stage 4: _____

Number of times
insect molts = _____

Incomplete Metamorphosis

_____
(name of insect)

Stage 1: _____

Stage 2: _____

Stage 3: _____

Number of times insect molts = _____

©2000 The Education Center, Inc. • _Investigating Science • Animals_ • TEC1731

Patterns

Use with "Jug Bug Mask" on page 25.

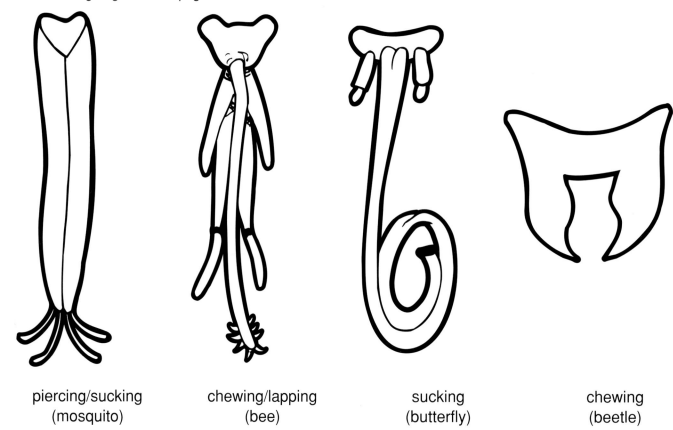

piercing/sucking
(mosquito)

chewing/lapping
(bee)

sucking
(butterfly)

chewing
(beetle)

- -

Use with "Insects Inside and Out" on page 26.

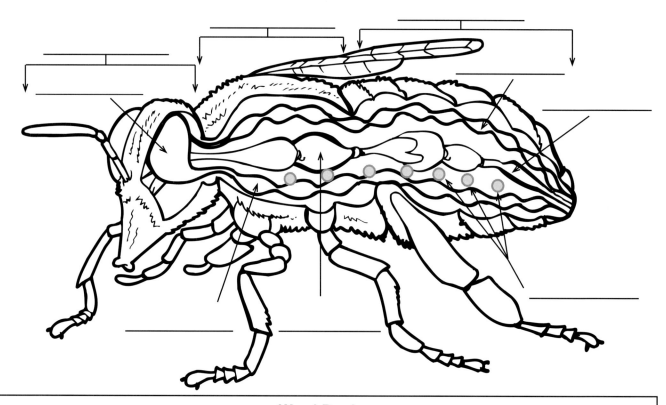

Word Bank
brain spiracles gizzard heart nervous system digestive system head thorax abdomen

Eyewitness Insect Log

Insect's Body:

Number of body parts _____

Number of legs _____

Number of wings _____

Number of antennae _____

Size _____

Other special features of the insect's body
(such as color) _____

_____

_____

_____

Getting Around:

Most of the time this insect moves by _____

_____ .

Sound:

This insect is quiet.

This insect makes a _____ noise.

Habitat:

I found this insect _____

_____ .

Social System: (circle one)

This insect seems to live alone.

This insect seems to live in a group.

Food:

I think this insect eats _____

_____ .

That's Cool!:

The most interesting thing about this insect is

_____ .

Sketch your insect in the magnifying glass.

Insect Name: _____

Endangered Animals

Heighten students' awareness of animals at risk and the laws protecting them with this collection of thought-provoking activities.

Endangered Animal Files
(Research)

Take students on a trek to find fabulous facts and interesting ideas about endangered animals. Divide students into groups of four or five. Give each group several magazines, scissors, glue, markers or crayons, and a file folder. Next, instruct each group to choose an endangered animal from the list on page 33. Direct each group to research to find the animal's habitat, its diet, its physical description, the steps being taken to preserve it, and other interesting information. Have each group use the magazines to find and cut out pictures relating to the information it has found, such as pictures of habitats, zoos, or animals. Instruct each group to create an endangered animal file by gluing the pictures and writing the information on the file folder as shown. Display folders on a file cabinet or bulletin board titled "Endangered Animal Files."

Background for the Teacher

- *Threatened* animal species include those animals whose numbers are low or declining. These animals are not in immediate danger of extinction, but will likely become endangered if they are not protected.
- *Endangered* animal species need protection to survive because they are in immediate danger of becoming extinct.
- *Extinct* is used to describe animal species that have died out completely.

Rare Reading Selections

The Atlas of Endangered Animals (Environmental Atlas series) by Steve Pollock (Facts on File, Inc.; 1993)

Can We Save Them? Endangered Species of North America by David Dobson (Charlesbridge Publishing, Inc.; 1997)

Macmillan Children's Guide to Endangered Animals by Roger Few (Macmillan Publishing Company, Inc.; 1993)

Jaguarundi by Virginia Hamilton (Scholastic Inc., 1995)

Ocean Animals in Danger (Survivors Series for Children) by Gary Turbak (Northland Publishing Company, 1994)

There's an Owl in the Shower by Jean Craighead George (HarperCollins Publishers, Inc.; 1997)

Will We Miss Them? Endangered Species (Nature's Treasures series) by Alexandra Wright (Charlesbridge Publishing, Inc.; 1992)

Endangered Ecosystems
(Research, Diagraming Ecosystems)

Give students insight into the world of endangered and extinct animals with this diagraming activity. Explain to students that an *ecosystem* is a system in which all living things depend on each other for survival. Point out that if an animal in an ecosystem becomes extinct or endangered, the ecosystem could be greatly affected because the natural balance of plants and animals would be disturbed. Next, give each student a sheet of 9" x 12" light-colored construction paper. Have the student fold the paper so the ends meet in the middle, making a pamphlet as shown. Then have each student choose an endangered animal from the list at the right. Direct the student to research his animal and its ecosystem. Instruct the student to use his researched information to draw a diagram on the outside of the pamphlet as shown. On the inside of the pamphlet, have each student write a paragraph explaining what might happen to the ecosystem's balance if the animal were to become extinct. Then have the student add illustrations. If desired, allow each student to share his pamphlet with the class.

Endangered Animals

manatee	American crocodile
ocelot	bald eagle
Florida panther	tiger
bighorn sheep	jaguar
blue whale	whooping crane
humpback whale	mountain lion
sperm whale	giant panda
gray wolf	orangutan
gibbon	giant armadillo
gorilla	brown bear
jaguarundi	bobcat
lemur	spider monkey
leopard	

The Florida Panther

If the Florida panther becomes extinct,

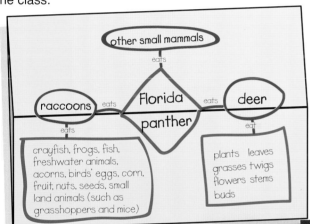

Endangered Elephants or Important Ivory?
(Debate)

The African elephant is one animal species that is in danger of extinction unless humans take action to protect it. Explain to students that habitat destruction and hunting in the 1970s and 1980s caused the number of elephants to decrease dramatically. During 1989, in an effort to help preserve the species, all trade in ivory and other elephant products was banned by the Convention on International Trade in Endangered Species of Wild Fauna and Flora (CITES). This ban helped reduce the number of African elephants being killed. However, in 1997, CITES decided to allow Namibia, Botswana, and Zimbabwe to resume exporting limited amounts of ivory to Japan. Brainstorm with students reasons CITES might have decided to lift the ban and the positive and negative results of its decision. Have students think about whether they agree or disagree with the CITES decision. Next, divide students into two teams, those in favor of the CITES decision and those against it. Instruct students to research the African elephant to find facts to support their positions. Then hold a class debate to help students understand both sides of the issue. After the debate, hold a secret vote to determine which viewpoint is held by a majority of the class.

Think Locally, Protect Globally
(Letter Writing, Art)

Challenge your students to learn more about the U.S. Fish and Wildlife Service in your area with this letter-writing activity. Explain to students that in 1973, the *Endangered Species Act* was passed by the U.S. government to protect disappearing plants and animals. According to the act, it is illegal to import, export, or sell animals protected by the act across state lines. The act also makes it illegal to harm protected animals, harass them, possess them, kill them, or take them from the wild without a special permit. The penalty for breaking this law can be a fine of up to $200,000 and/or a year in jail. The Endangered Species Act further states that it is the responsibility of the U.S. Fish and Wildlife Service to protect endangered and threatened species and their habitats. With students, write a letter to the U.S. Fish and Wildlife office in your area. (See chart above.) Ask if there are any local animal species that are threatened or endangered and, if so, what is being done to help them in their environments. Then have each student use the information received to design a 3-D educational poster promoting the protection of these animal species as shown. If desired, display students' posters in local businesses to increase community awareness.

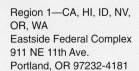

Addresses for the U.S. Fish and Wildlife Service

Region 1—CA, HI, ID, NV, OR, WA
Eastside Federal Complex
911 NE 11th Ave.
Portland, OR 97232-4181

Region 2—AZ, NM, OK, TX
P.O. Box 1306
500 Gold Ave.
Albuquerque, NM 87103

Region 3—IL, IN, IA, MI, MN, MO, OH, WI
Bishop Henry Federal Building
One Federal Dr.
Fort Snelling, MN 55111-4056

Region 4—AL, AR, FL, GA, KY, LA, MS, NC, SC, TN
1875 Century Blvd.
Suite 200
Atlanta, GA 30345

Region 5—CT, DE, ME, MD, MA, NH, NJ, NY, PA, RI, VT, VA, WV
300 Westgate Center Dr.
Hadley, MA 01035

Region 6—CO, KS, MT, NE, ND, SD, UT, WY
P.O. Box 25486
Denver Federal Center
Denver, CO 80225

Region 7—AK
1011 E. Tudor Rd.
Anchorage, AK 99503

Washington D.C. Office
Division of Endangered Species
(MS-452 ARLSQ)
1849 C St., NW
Washington, DC 20240

SAVE THE AMERICAN CROCODILE!

Be careful when boating!

Don't buy crocodile-skin boots!

Wild About Refuges
(Research, Art, Descriptive Writing)

The National Wildlife Refuge System in the United States includes over 92 million acres of land and water set aside for the conservation of fish, wildlife, and plants. One of the goals of the National Wildlife Refuge System is "to preserve, restore, and enhance in their natural ecosystems (when practicable) all species of animals and plants that are endangered or threatened with becoming endangered." A week before beginning this project, have students bring in shoeboxes or cereal boxes. Next, challenge your students to imagine that they have been asked to design a wildlife refuge that will protect a specific threatened or endangered animal species. Direct each student to select an animal she would like to protect. Then have the student research her animal's habitat and diet. Have the student use the information she collects to create a shoebox diorama of what her wildlife refuge would look like. Instruct the student to write a descriptive paragraph about her refuge and attach it to her display. If desired, allow each student to share her diorama and paragraph with the class. Then display students' dioramas on a table titled "Wild About Refuges."

The Road to Endangerment

Have you ever wondered why animals become endangered? Get on the road to understanding endangerment by completing the following activity.

Part 1: Read the list of reasons animals become endangered. Then read the descriptions of how each animal may be riding down the road to endangerment in the boxes below. Write the letter of the reason the animal is endangered in the blank. **Hint:** Letters can be used more than once.

Reasons Animals Become Endangered

A. habitat loss
B. unregulated or illegal killing or collection of animals

C. pesticides/pollution
D. predators
E. disease

---

1. Tourism has left fewer and fewer beaches on which the Mediterranean monk seal can breed.

   _____

2. The bald eagle ate fish contaminated with chemicals.

   _____

---

3. The eggs and young of the spotted salamander are being killed by acid rain.

   _____

4. The red-kneed tarantula has become an exotic and popular pet.

   _____

   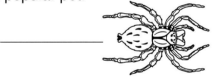

---

5. Wetlands, the whooping crane's habitat, have been drained off to make way for farms and city growth.

   _____

   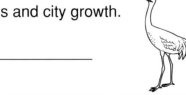

6. A dangerous parasite infects the Gouldian finch.

   _____

---

7. Tiger fur has been used to make rugs and coats.

   _____

8. Foxes, cats, and dogs introduced by settlers preyed on the numbat.

   _____

Part 2: Research to find one animal different from those listed above that is endangered or threatened because of each one of the causes listed. Write them on the back of this sheet.

Interview With an Extinct Animal

Ernie X. Tinkshun, a reporter for the local newspaper, was out one day tracking a story when he came upon an animal that had been classified as extinct. He decided to stop and interview this creature. Help Ernie write his notes and newspaper article by following the directions below.

Directions: Read and choose one animal species from the extinct animal list shown. Research to find the answers to the following questions. Then write the answers in the form of a newspaper article in the space provided.

Extinct Animals

dodo

heath hen

passenger pigeon

moa (giant flightless bird)

mammoth

saber-toothed cat

Steller's sea cow

Tasmanian tiger

great auk

archaeopteryx

Questions

1. What is the name of your species?
2. When did scientists first claim that your species was extinct?
3. Where have you been all this time?
4. What have you been eating?
5. What predators have been after you? How did you escape from them?
6. Did humans have anything to do with your species dying out?
7. What could have been done to prevent your species from becoming extinct?
8. What will you do now that you are the only one of your species left? Where will you live? What will you eat?

_____

(Title)

Illustration (you and your animal)

Policing Our World

Help put a stop to the steady decline of our world's animals. Complete the following activity to see how you can help!

Directions: Read the descriptions of how to help certain endangered animals. Match each animal illustrated at the bottom of the page with the appropriate way it can be helped. Cut out each illustration and paste it onto the box beside its description.

1. Do not buy jewelry made from shells.

2. Do not play in or vandalize caves.

3. Refuse to buy products made from this animal's horn.

4. Refuse to buy products, such as shoes and purses, made from this animal's skin.

5. Learn about large cats, so you won't be afraid and feel the need to kill them.

6. Build special nests on rooftops of big buildings, complete with landing strips and gravel to keep eggs from rolling away.

7. Refuse to buy products made from ivory.

8. Be careful about how much water you use.

9. Write letters to government officials asking for more protected land, like open meadows and river valleys, for these big animals.

10. Encourage people in motorboats to slow down while driving through this animal's habitat.

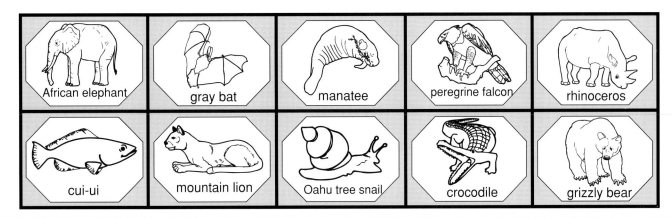

African elephant   gray bat   manatee   peregrine falcon   rhinoceros

cui-ui   mountain lion   Oahu tree snail   crocodile   grizzly bear

Animal Adaptations

Walk, swim, fly, or run into the world of animal adaptations with this collection of adaptable activities and reproducibles!

Background for the Teacher

- *Adaptation* refers to the ability of living things to adjust to different conditions within their environments. An animal must adapt to its environment in order to survive.
- A *structural adaptation* involves some part of an animal's body, such as the size or shape of the teeth, the animal's body covering, or the way the animal moves.
- *Protective coloration* and *protective resemblance* allow an animal to blend in with its environment.
- *Mimicry* allows one animal to look, sound, or act like another animal to fool predators into thinking it is poisonous or dangerous.
- *Behavioral adaptations* include activities that help an animal survive. Behavioral adaptations can be learned or *instinctive* (a behavior an animal is born with).
- *Migration* is a behavioral adaptation that involves an animal or group of animals moving from one region to another and then back again.
- *Hibernation* is a deep sleep in which an animal's body temperature drops to about the temperature of the environment. Body activities, such as heartbeat and breathing, are slowed, causing the animal to need very little food.

Need to Adapt?
(Research, Making a Mobile)

Help students understand the many types of animal adaptations with this mobile-making activity. Explain to students that animals must adapt to changes in their environments in order to survive. For example, a snowshoe hare changes color with the seasons so that it can blend in with its environment. Write the different types of adaptations listed below on a chalkboard or chart paper. Give each student scissors, one sheet of 12" x 18" construction paper, one clothes hanger, and string. Next, have each student choose one adaptation and then research it to find several animals that have that adaptation. Instruct each student to construct a mobile, as shown, featuring the adaptation and the animals. If desired, hang students' mobiles from the ceiling to create an awesome animal display!

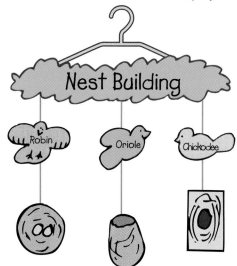

Amazing Animal Adaptations Booklist

Animal Defenses: How Animals Protect Themselves by Etta Kaner (Kids Can Press Ltd., 1999)

Armor to Venom: Animal Defenses (First Book series) by Phyllis J. Perry (Franklin Watts, Inc.; 1997)

Beaks and Noses (Head to Tail series) by Theresa Greenaway (Raintree Steck-Vaughn Publishers, 1995)

Questions and Answers About Polar Animals by Michael Chinery (Kingfisher Books, 1994)

Adaptations

teeth—incisors, molars, canines
mouthparts—tube, beak
movement—wings, powerful arms and legs
coverings—moist skin, hair, armor
coloration—color is similar to surroundings
resemblance—looks similar to something in surroundings
mimicry—looks like a dangerous or poisonous animal
defenses—escaping, fighting
nest building—building different types of nests
hibernation—deep sleep
migration—moving back and forth region to region
practice—repeating the process
reinforcement—punishment or reward given
imprinting—learning caused by one experience that estab-
    lishes a pattern

Creature Features
(Research, Center Activity)

Learning about adaptations is in the bag with this creative center activity! Assign each student a different number and an animal from the box below, keeping a master list as you go. (Use this list as an answer key.) Then give each student a paper bag and five strips of paper. Have the student write her number on the front of her bag. On each strip of paper, have the student write one sentence about her animal's adaptations without stating the name of the animal. Then have the student place the completed strips in her bag. Arrange the completed bags, along with the directions below and a copy of the answer key, in a center titled "Creature Features."

Directions:

1. Number a sheet of paper from 1 to the number of bags displayed.
2. Choose a bag, remove the clues, and read each one.
3. Decide which animal you think the clues represent. Then write the name of the animal described next to its corresponding number on your paper.
4. Return the strips to the bag and choose another bag.
5. Continue in this manner until you have examined all of the bags and filled in all of the animal names on your paper.
6. Use the answer key to check the number of animals you guessed correctly.

> It can stay underwater for three or four minutes.

> This animal is an expert swimmer.

> It has a layer of fat that insulates it from the cold.

> It can use its paws to handle objects, such as stones and small shellfish.

> It has elastic webbing between its toes.

Animals			
bighorn sheep	moose	driver ant	snowy owl
golden eagle	otter	dingo	emperor penguin
chinchilla	spotted owl	roadrunner	killer whale
giraffe	ocelot	scorpion	manatee
ostrich	spider monkey	Arctic hare	octopus
eland	two-toed sloth	polar bear	purple sea urchin
aardvark	tarantula	musk ox	jellyfish

Migrating Math
(Using a Scale, Graphing)

Get students on the road to learning about migration with this math activity! Post the migration distances below on a chalkboard or sheet of chart paper. Next, divide students into groups of four. Instruct each group to create a scale, such as four trips around the playground equals one mile. Then have each group convert the migration distances on a sheet of paper, using its scale. For example, 250 trips around the playground equals the caribou's migratory journey. Discuss students' findings. Conclude the activity by having each group create a bar graph comparing the migration of each animal.

Migration Distances
pink salmon—about 7,000 miles
green sea turtle—about 2,800 miles
Arctic tern—about 24,000 miles
wildebeest—about 380 miles
North American monarch butterfly—about 4,000 miles
North American caribou—about 1,000 miles
Mexican free-tailed bat—about 1,600 miles

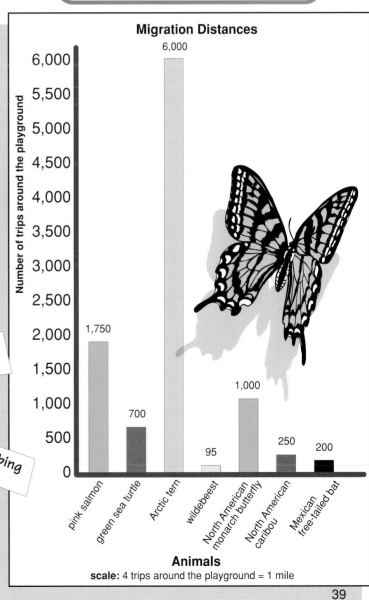

Migration Distances

Number of trips around the playground

- pink salmon — 1,750
- green sea turtle — 700
- Arctic tern — 6,000
- wildebeest — 95
- North American monarch butterfly — 1,000
- North American caribou — 250
- Mexican free-tailed bat — 200

Animals
scale: 4 trips around the playground = 1 mile

39

Amazing Adaptations
(Research, Making Quadramas)

Further students' study of animal adaptations with this crafty quadrama activity. Have each student choose an animal from the list on page 39. Direct the student to research his animal to find out how it has adapted to its environment. Next, provide each student with the materials listed below. Then divide students into groups of four. Guide each group through the following steps to make a quadrama about its animals' habitats and adaptations. If desired, allow each group to share its quadrama, explaining the animals' adaptations. Hang students' quadramas in the library for other classes to enjoy!

Materials for each student: one 9" x 9" sheet of light construction paper, one 8½" x 11" sheet of white construction paper, scissors, glue, markers, tape

Steps:
1. Fold a 9" x 9" sheet of paper diagonally as shown in Figure 1.
2. Open and cut along one fold line, stopping at the center as shown in Figure 2.
3. Illustrate your animal's habitat on the top two triangles as shown in Figure 3.
4. Overlap the two bottom triangles of each square and secure them with glue or tape as shown in Figure 4.
5. Use markers and scissors to create and cut out construction paper stand-up animals and plants to make the habitat three-dimensional as shown in Figure 5.
6. Glue the back of your scene to the backs of the other group members' scenes, creating a quadrama as shown in Figure 6.

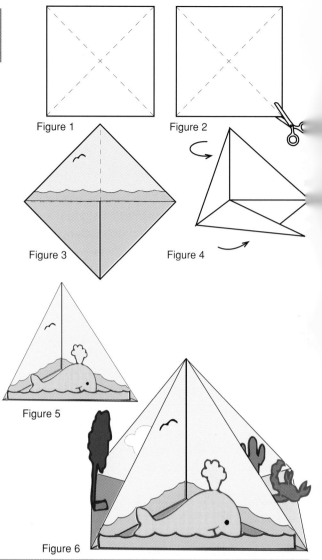

Figure 1

Figure 2

Figure 3

Figure 4

Figure 5

Figure 6

What If Fish Had Feet?
(Creative Thinking, Art)

Challenge students to use the information they have gathered about animal adaptations with this creative-thinking activity. In advance, have students bring in shoeboxes or cereal boxes. Show students a picture of a bird and discuss the importance of its adaptations, such as its wing span, type of feathers, and type of beak. Next, brainstorm other animal adaptations, such as types of protective coverings and behaviors. Discuss with students what would happen if an animal didn't have an adaptation it needed or had an extra adaptation, such as a bird without feathers or a fish with feet. How would these changes help and/or harm the animal? Get students to think further about extra adaptations by reading *Imogene's Antlers* by David Small (Crown Publishers, Inc.; 1986), a story about a girl who wakes up one morning with antlers. Direct each student to choose an animal; then have her create a shoebox diorama showing the animal with an extra or missing adaptation as shown. Instruct the student to also show any changes in the animal's habitat. If desired, display students' dioramas in an area titled "What If Fish Had Feet?"

Adapt-a-Lotto
(Adaptation Game)

Add adaptations to the game of lotto for a quick and easy review! Give each student a copy of the animal adaptations and gameboard below and nine beans or markers. Instruct each student to choose nine adaptations and write one in each square on her gameboard. Next, read aloud one of the following adaptation clues. Direct any student who has the adaptation described on her gameboard to cover it with a bean. Continue to read the clues in this manner until one student has covered a horizontal, vertical, or diagonal row and yells out "Adapt-a-Lotto!" Check the student's gameboard before declaring a winner. If desired, play again, directing students to fill two horizontal or vertical rows, the four corners, or the whole board to win.

Clues:

Salamanders stay underground during cold weather. *(hibernation)*

Gray whales spend the summer in the Bering Sea and the fall in Baja California. *(migration)*

A frilled lizard raises its special folds of skin, making an attacker think it is larger. *(fright)*

The viceroy butterfly is often mistaken for the poisonous monarch butterfly. *(mimicry)*

A walking stick looks a lot like the branches on which it lives. *(protective resemblance)*

The chameleon turns green when it is on green leaves. *(protective coloration)*

The Goliath beetle can't run fast, but it has a thick armor. *(body covering)*

The butterfly has a *proboscis,* shaped like a drinking straw, which helps it get nectar from flowers. *(special mouthparts)*

A skunk squirts a horrible-smelling liquid on its attacker. *(chemical defense)*

Caribou have antlers that are large enough to fend off grizzly bears. *(special weapons)*

A gibbon stays off the ground. It spends its entire life in the trees. *(avoidance)*

An impala can run at a speed of 50 miles per hour. *(escape)*

Musk oxen defend their calves by standing in a circle with their horns facing outward. *(group defense)*

A North American opossum closes its eyes and becomes totally limp in the presences of an enemy. *(playing dead)*

Adapt-a-Lotto Gameboard

Animal Adaptations

mimicry
avoidance
special mouthparts
chemical defense
escape
protective coloration
protective resemblance
body covering
group defense
special weapons
hibernation
fright
playing dead
migration

Habitat Hunt

Agent Aardvark is on a hunt to determine how different animals protect themselves in their habitats. Help the agent assemble his data by following the directions below.

Directions: Use a ruler to draw a line between each animal and its habitat. On the lines following, write a phrase explaining the adaptations the animal has in order to live in its habitat. Then answer the riddle at the bottom of the page by writing the letters that the lines cross in the correct spaces.

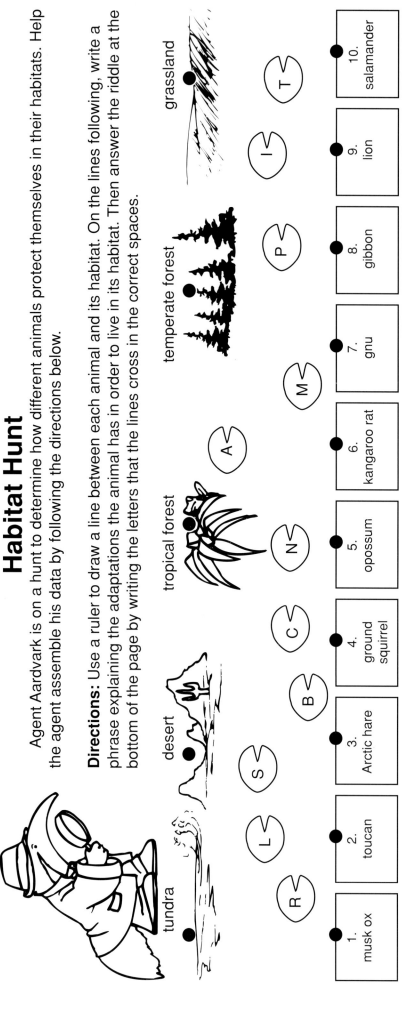

tundra •
desert •
tropical forest •
temperate forest •
grassland •

(R) (L) (S) (B) (C) (N) (A) (M) (P) (I) (T)

1. • musk ox
2. • toucan
3. • Arctic hare
4. • ground squirrel
5. • opossum
6. • kangaroo rat
7. • gnu
8. • gibbon
9. • lion
10. • salamander

1. _____
2. _____
3. _____
4. _____
5. _____
6. _____
7. _____
8. _____
9. _____
10. _____

What does the buffalo think of his habitat?

He thinks it's rather

___ ___ ___ ___ ___ ___ !
 7   3   8 10   6

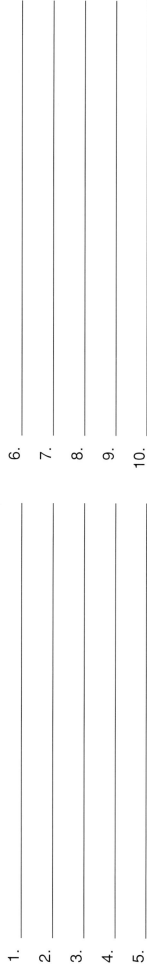

©2000 The Education Center, Inc. • *Investigating Science • Animals* • TEC1731 • Key p. 48

Name _____

Surfing the Wildlife Web!

Professor Wyle D. Animal is surfing the Web for sites with never-before-seen wildlife. Follow the directions below to design a Web page that will really get the professor's attention.

Directions:

1. Choose a habitat from the list below.
2. Using the questions as a guide, create a new animal that could survive in the habitat you've chosen. Then draw the new animal on the computer screen at the bottom of the page.
3. Enhance your Web page by adding words and illustrations that tell about your animal and its habitat.

Habitats
mountains
grasslands
temperate forests
tropical forests
deserts
polar regions
oceans

Questions
What adaptations does your animal have to survive?
What type of shelter does it need?
Does it hibernate or migrate?
What does it eat?
What enemies does it have?
What other interesting characteristics does it have?

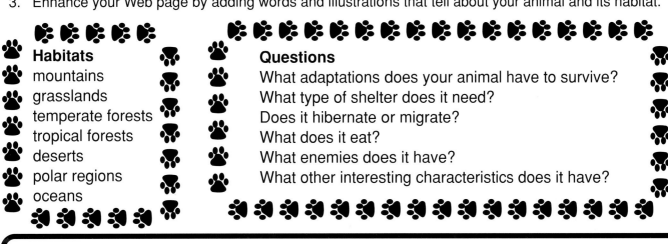

Address: http://www. _____ .com

_____
(Title)

Food Chains and Food Webs

Make learning about food chains and food webs a picnic with these appetizing activities!

Background for the Teacher

- A *food chain* shows how energy passes from one *organism* (living thing) to another.
- Food chains always begin with a *producer* (green plant). Producers use water, carbon dioxide, and sunlight to make their own food.
- A *consumer* is an organism that eats other organisms for energy. There are three general categories of consumers: *herbivore* (eats plants only), *carnivore* (eats animals only), and *omnivore* (eats both plants and animals).
- Some animals eat dead plants and animals. *Scavengers,* such as vultures, eat dead animals; *decomposers,* such as worms, feed on dead material (plants and animals).
- *Parasites,* such as ticks and fleas, feed on living organisms, called *hosts.* While *predators,* such as lions, kill and eat their *prey* (zebras), parasites use their hosts as a continual source of food.
- Food chains that overlap are called *food webs.* Food webs show how all the living things in an *ecosystem,* a community of living organisms and their nonliving environment, interact with and depend on one another for survival.

Making Connections
(Vocabulary, Classification)

Help students make connections with food chains in a colorful way. Copy the color code shown onto the board. Divide students into groups of four. Provide each group with 1¹/₂" x 9" strips of green, blue, red, and purple construction paper, a stapler, and a list of plants and animals (see chart). Next, introduce some important food chain vocabulary: *producer, herbivore, carnivore,* and *omnivore* (see background information on this page). Then have each group use the paper strips and the color code to make a paper food chain. Instruct students to label each strip with the name of a plant or animal from each category and then staple the links in the order they appear in the food chain (see example). Invite groups to share their discoveries. Have students listen for common links among groups in order to link together food webs. Finally, use the chains to discuss how the removal of a link might affect animals and plants in a food chain.

Color Code
green—producer (green plant)
blue—herbivore (eats plants)
red—carnivore (eats animals)
purple—omnivore (eats plants and animals)

Producer: lettuce, tree/leaf, grass, berry, green plant, phytoplankton
Herbivore: rabbit, lemming, musk ox, caribou, zooplankton, giraffe, zebra, antelope, squirrel, deer, cow
Carnivore: weasel, badger, lynx, wolf, coral, sponge, moray eel, pufferfish, shark, barracuda, squid, butterfly fish, arctic tern, walrus, polar bear, fox, seal, krill, small fish, beluga, cheetah, hyena, leopard, lion, vulture, jackal, anteater, owl
Omnivore: human, bear, mouse, ostrich, ant, crossbill (bird), parrotfish, damselfish

Linking Food Chains and Literature

Food Chains (Straightforward Science series) by Peter Riley (Franklin Watts, Inc.; 1998)

The Hunt for Food (Life's Cycles series) by Anita Ganeri (The Millbrook Press, Inc.; 1997)

Pass the Energy, Please! (Sharing Nature With Children series) by Barbara Shaw McKinney (Dawn Publications, 2000)

Red Fox Running by Eve Bunting (Clarion Books, 1996)

This Is the Sea That Feeds Us by Robert F. Baldwin (Dawn Publications, 1998)

What Are Food Chains and Webs? (The Science of Living Things series) by Bobbie Kalman and Jacqueline Langille (Crabtree Publishing Company, 1998)

Pass the Pyramid!
(Vocabulary Review, Game)

Use this idea to actively review vocabulary. Before beginning, provide each student with glue, scissors, and a copy of page 46. Assign each student a food chain word (see "Food Chain Vocabulary"). Have the student use another sheet of paper to write four words or phrases that are clues related to his assigned vocabulary word. Next, have him transfer his words or phrases to the pyramid pattern on page 46—one word or phrase on each of the four triangles and the vocabulary word and his name on the square. Then have him illustrate each of his clues. Finally, tell him to follow the directions on page 46 to construct his pyramid (see sample). To play the review game, bring along some music and follow the steps below.

To play the game:
1. Have students form a large circle.
2. Play music while students pass one of the pyramids from student to student.
3. Stop the music.
4. Have whoever is holding the pyramid when the music stops read aloud the clues on the pyramid and try to guess the word being described.
5. If the student doesn't guess correctly, ask the class. Anyone may answer except for the person who made that pyramid.
6. Have the student check the answer on the bottom of the pyramid.
7. Continue to play in this manner with each of the remaining pyramids.

Marvelous Menus!
(Creative Thinking and Writing, Alliteration)

Reinforce food chain facts and have fun with alliteration too! Divide the class into three groups. Assign each group one of the three types of consumers: herbivores, omnivores, or carnivores. Then provide each group with one sheet of poster board and markers. Explain to students that each group will be making a menu for a restaurant in which members of its consumer group might be the patrons. Next, have the group brainstorm the kinds of food its patrons would eat. For example, herbivores eat only dishes made from plants. Tell students to use *alliteration* when writing their menus. (Remind them that alliteration is repeating the initial consonant sounds of words or syllables that are near each other.) When all groups are finished, have them share their completed menus with the class.

The Herbivore Hash House

Today's Specials!
Crispy Carrots
Appetizing Apples
Sassy Sunflower Seeds
Bunches of Bermuda Grass

Food Chain Vocabulary

carnivore	omnivore	host
food chain	food web	consumer
parasite	energy	predator
decomposer	prey	herbivore
producer	ecosystem	top predator
secondary consumer	photosynthesis	tertiary consumer
carrion	phytoplankton	zooplankton
krill	detritus food web	chlorophyll
		scavenger

Pattern

Use with "Pass the Pyramid!" on page 45.

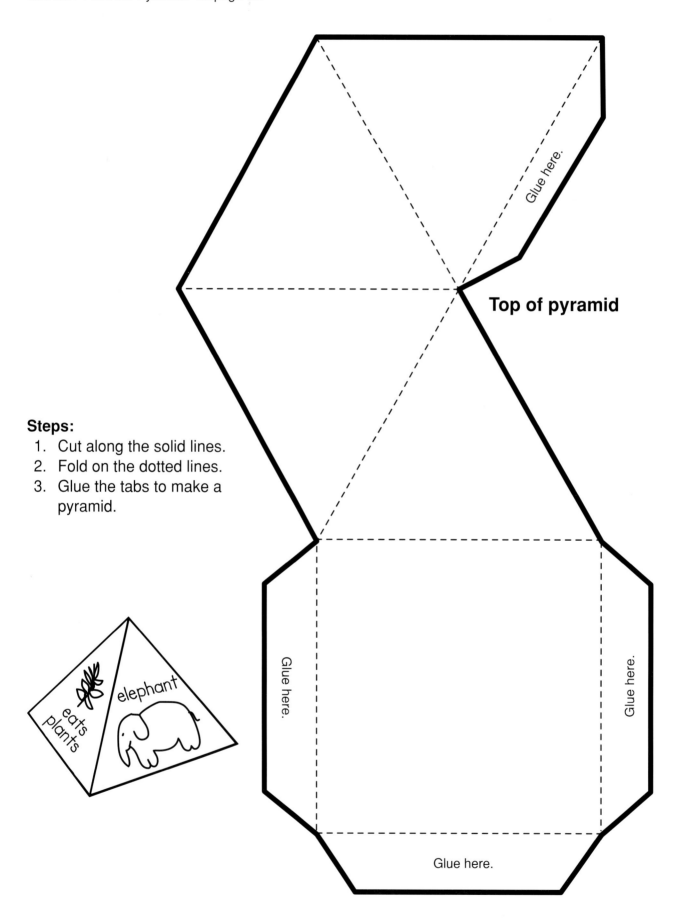

Top of pyramid

Glue here.

Glue here.

Glue here.

Glue here.

eats plants

elephant

Steps:

1. Cut along the solid lines.
2. Fold on the dotted lines.
3. Glue the tabs to make a pyramid.

Context Connections

These two chatty cheetahs are having a hard time understanding the facts about food chains because they don't understand the vocabulary. Help clear up their confusion by completing the following activity.

Directions: Read the sentences below. Use the context clue found in each sentence to match the vocabulary word with a definition. Write the letter of the definition in the appropriate blank beside each sentence.

_____ 1. All plants and animals need the **energy** they get from food to survive.

_____ 2. Green plants "eat" through the process of **photosynthesis.**

_____ 3. Some plants do not get all the nutrients they need from the soil, so they **consume** insects.

_____ 4. All animals are **consumers.** They cannot make their own food.

_____ 5. The vegetarians of the animal kingdom are called **herbivores.**

_____ 6. In most ecosystems, **omnivores** do not have a problem finding enough food because they eat almost anything they find.

_____ 7. A small food chain forms when zooplankton, tiny water animals, graze on **phytoplankton.**

_____ 8. Each type of **predator** has a different way of catching food, such as stalking or tracking.

_____ 9. Some predators set traps for their **prey,** such as building a sticky web.

_____10. **Scavengers** help keep an ecosystem clean by eating the leftovers from a predator's meal.

A
animal that hunts and kills other animals for food

B
animals that feed on dead animal flesh

C
eat

D
power needed to do things

E
living things that eat other living things for energy

F
living things that eat plants

G
process that traps the sun's energy and stores it in the form of food

H
tiny plants that live in water

I
living things that eat both plants and animals

J
animal that is hunted and eaten by another animal

Bonus Box: Write a short paragraph describing how you are a part of a food chain.

Answer Keys

Page 11
1. blue whale
2. red fox
3. Tasmanian devil
4. reindeer
5. gray squirrel
6. brown bear
7. black panther
8. African elephant
9. killer whale
10. snowshoe hare

Page 12
1. Arctic tern
2. no
3. white-fronted goose
4. barn swallow
5. Arctic tern, lesser golden plover, white stork, barn swallow
6. lesser golden plover
7. white-fronted goose
8. five

Page 15
Students' fish pictures will vary.
More than 95 percent of all fish are bony fish. *Modern bony fish* have skeletons made from bone. They live in freshwater and saltwater. *Primitive bony fish* have skeletons made from bone and cartilage. These fish live mainly in freshwater.

Cartilaginous fish have skeletons of tough cartilage. There are about 790 species of cartilaginous fish. These fish mainly live in saltwater.

Jawless fish are divided into two groups: lampreys and hagfish. These fish have funnel-shaped sucking mouths and lack proper gills. Lampreys live in freshwater and saltwater, and hagfish live only in saltwater.

Page 22
Role 1: Ellen Echinodermata
Role 2: Molly Mollusca
Role 3: Arthur Arthropoda
Role 4: Annie Annelida
Role 5: Paul Platyhelminthes
Role 6: Polly Porifera
Role 7: Sid Coelenterate
Role 8: Nan Nematoda

Page 23

A = 69	N = 64	1.	one million
B = 52	O = 68	2.	scorpion
C = 78	P = 354	3.	clam
D = 96	Q = 435	4.	jellyfish
E = 87	R = 76	5.	sponge
F = 195	S = 84	6.	worms
G = 70	T = 54	7.	starfish
H = 63	U = 336	8.	sea anemone
I = 231	V = 196	9.	tube feet
J = 91	W = 486	10.	lobster
K = 351	X = 99		
L = 144	Y = 72		
M = 168	Z = 395		

Page 35
Part 1:
1. A
2. C
3. C
4. B
5. A
6. E
7. B
8. D

Part 2: Answers will vary.

Page 37
1. Oahu tree snail
2. gray bat
3. rhinoceros
4. crocodile
5. mountain lion
6. peregrine falcon
7. African elephant
8. cui-ui
9. grizzly bear
10. manatee

Page 42
1. musk ox—tundra
2. toucan—tropical forest
3. Arctic hare—tundra
4. ground squirrel—desert
5. opossum—temperate forest
6. kangaroo rat—desert
7. gnu—grassland
8. gibbon—tropical forest
9. lion—grassland
10. salamander—temperate forest

Adaptation examples may vary. Accept reasonable responses.
1. thick fur to keep it warm
2. wings to fly from tree to tree
3. short ears and short tail to keep in body heat
4. *estivates,* or sleeps through the summer, to keep cool
5. small body to move easily through the underbrush
6. spends days in a burrow to keep cool
7. ability to travel long distances to find grass to eat
8. long arms used to swing from tree to tree
9. sharp canine teeth for killing and then tearing prey
10. hides under leaves and rocks to find and eat insects

Riddle answer: He thinks it's rather p l a i n !

Page 47
1. D
2. G
3. C
4. E
5. F
6. I
7. H
8. A
9. J
10. B

Bonus Box: Answers will vary. Accept reasonable responses.